GERRARD WINSTANLEY

This essential new series features classic texts by key figures that took centre stage during a period of insurrection. Each book is introduced by a major contemporary radical writer who shows how these incendiary words still have the power to inspire, to provoke and maybe to ignite new revolutions . . .

1

Also available:

Sheila Rowbotham presents Mary Wollstonecraft:
A Vindication of the Rights of Woman

Wu Ming presents Thomas Müntzer:
The Sermon to the Princes

Hugo Chávez presents Simón Bolívar:
The Bolívarian Revolution

Dr Jean-Bertrand Aristide presents Toussaint L'Ouverture:
The Haitian Revolution

Slavoj Žižek presents Trotsky:
Terrorism and Communism

Michael Hardt presents Thomas Jefferson:
The Declaration of Independence

Slavoj Žižek presents Mao:
On Practice and Contradiction

Walden Bello presents Ho Chi Minh:
Down with Colonialism!

Alain Badiou presents Marx:
The Civil War in France

Tariq Ali presents Castro:
The Declarations of Havana

Slavoj Žižek presents Robespierre:
Virtue and Terror

Terry Eagleton presents Jesus Christ:
The Gospels

Geoffrey Robertson presents The Levellers:
The Putney Debates

TONY BENN PRESENTS

A COMMON TREASURY

◆

GERRARD WINSTANLEY

EDITED AND SELECTED BY ANDREW HOPTON
WITH A FOREWORD AND ANNOTATIONS BY TOM
HAZELDINE

VERSO
London • New York

First published by Verso 2011
Selection and text originally published as *Gerrard Winstanley:
Selected Writings*, edited by Andrew Hopton
© Aporia Press 1989

Foreword © Tom Hazeldine 2011
Introduction © Tony Benn 2011

1 3 5 7 9 10 8 6 4 2

Verso
UK: 6 Meard Street, London W1F 0EG
US: 20 Jay Street, Suite 1010, Brooklyn, NY 11201
www.versobooks.com

Verso is the imprint of New Left Books

ISBN-13: 978-1-84467-595-1

British Library Cataloguing in Publication Data
A catalogue record for this book is available from the British Library

Library of Congress Cataloging-in-Publication Data
A catalog record for this book is available from the Library of Congress

Typeset in Bembo by Hewer Text UK Ltd, Edinburgh
Printed in the US by Maple Vail

Contents

Foreword

by Tom Hazeldine

Oliver Cromwell once remarked something to the effect that 'none goes so far as he who knows not whither he is going'.[1] The English Civil War amply illustrates the point. That the parliamentary campaign against Charles I should have resulted in the surrender of political initiative to an independent and radical New Model Army, a military occupation of London and purge of Westminster, and the trial and execution of the king, was not at all anticipated at the outset. What would happen to the new republic, still in gestation when the Diggers emerged in the spring of 1649, was similarly unclear. Gerrard Winstanley's entire corpus dates to this turbulent period around the end of the war, when he acted as instigator and apologist for the short-lived but notorious Digger commune of St George's Hill. The bulk of the Digger writings are reproduced in this volume.

These were heady days in England's Revolution. The first Digger manifesto, *The True Levellers Standard Advanced*, memorably described 'the old world' as 'running up like parchment in the fire, and wearing away'. Charles I had gone to the scaffold on 30 January 1649, after Cromwell's victory at Preston the previous summer had precluded a royalist revival. The Rump Parliament, remnant of the Army's December purge, now abolished the monarchy and House of Lords. What other wonders might the Civil War leave in its wake? With renewed Leveller agitation, mutiny in the ranks, and a population in dire straits, it seemed the Revolution had not yet come to rest; radicals like Winstanley could hope to produce far-reaching effects.[2]

The Digger colony of St George's Hill commenced on 1 April 1649, when Winstanley and a handful of confederates stole onto waste land in Walton-on-Thames, Surrey, and began to sow parsnips, carrots and beans. In the following days they fired part of the heath, purchased seed-corn, and set to ploughing. 'The Work we are going about is this,' explained *The True Levellers Standard Advanced*: 'To dig up *Georges-Hill* and the waste Ground thereabouts, and to Sow Corn, and to eat our bread together by the sweat of our brows.' The manifesto rejected the 'peculier Interest of Lords and Landlords' to the land. When Winstanley and his comrade William Everard stood before Sir Thomas Fairfax, the Lord General, on 20 April – without removing their hats, since 'he was but their fellow-creature' – Everard reportedly declared that

> he was of the race of the Jews; that all the liberties of the people were lost by the coming in of William the Conqueror, and that ever since, the people of God had lived under tyranny and oppression worse than that of our forefathers under the Egyptians. But now the time of the deliverance was at hand ... That as God had promised to make the barren land fruitful, so now what they did was to renew the ancient community of enjoying the fruits of the earth, and to distribute the benefit thereof to the poor and needy.[3]

What are we to make of this behaviour, and of the Digger enterprise as a whole? We know the names of seventy-four adherents; one-third were local to the area, many from neighbouring Cobham. 'The Cobham Diggers were not all from among the poorest sections of the population,' observes John Gurney, 'but most appear to have been on the fringes of local society'. The Digger movement 'attracted middling sorts as well as poor, and in its social composition it thus showed similarities to early Quakerism'.[4] Everard was a colourful character, a former radical in the New Model Army cashiered after the 1647 mutiny at Ware. Winstanley defended him against a charge of blasphemy in 1648. Everard soon left the colony to join a Berkshire community associated with the Family of Love, an underground mystic sect brought over from the Netherlands around 1550. He is last heard of in Bethlem.[5]

Winstanley's career, excluding for the moment his Digger period, was decidedly more mundane. Born into the textile trade in Wigan in 1609, he moved to London as an apprentice in 1630 and became a freeman of the Merchant Taylors Company in 1638. Soon afterwards he married the daughter of a London surgeon. Wartime disruption bankrupted his 'small-scale and precarious business, most probably buying cloth wholesale for resale', in 1643.[6] Winstanley recounts how he was 'beaten out both of estate and trade, and forced to accept of the good will of friends crediting of me, to live a Countrey-life'.[7] He moved to Cobham – where his father-in-law held substantial property by the 1650s – and herded cows for a living. His post-Digger life brought a return to respectability. He undertook the usual local offices in Cobham such as churchwarden and high constable. It seems he became a corn-chandler. By 1675 he had relocated to London, 'living in comfort in a substantial house in already fashionable Bloomsbury'.[8] He died in 1676.

Winstanley launched into print in 1648, only a year before the Diggers got under way. Four theological tracts appeared in quick succession. In one of them Winstanley confesses to a Baptist background; he had at some point undergone the 'ordinance of dipping'.[9] By 1648, however, he had passed far beyond Anabaptism into an intense spiritualism and mysticism. 'Many things were revealed to me which I never read in books', he later claimed.[10] This was not so surprising in a period of great religious excitability. Sectarians and mystics of various stripes, among them the antinomian Ranters disowned by Winstanley, exploited the collapse of ecclesiastical discipline and censorship to emerge from hiding. Erstwhile progressives in the Commons had cause to lament the 'general increase of open libertinism, secret atheism, bold Arminianism, desperate Socinianism, stupid Anabaptism' which openly contested the dour rationalism and social conservatism of Cromwell's puritans.[11] Winstanley's early works advance a 'spiritual interpretation of history' also present in his Digger writings, but in *The New Law of Righteousness*, published in January 1649, he expanded 'from the misty regions of cosmological, metaphysical and theistical speculations to the somewhat firmer ground of social thought'.[12] The text cleared the way to the Digger commune by developing several key themes: condemnation of trade in land, belief that private ownership translates into a certain type of – tyrannical – politics, and advocacy of a return to primitive communism through the mass withdrawal of labour from the enclosed lands of the rich to the commons of the poor.[13]

The Diggers, self-styled 'True Levellers', took their coordinates from the Leveller reform movement whipped up by London pamphleteers affiliated to radicals in the New Model.[14] There was certainly a degree of overlap between them: a shared disappointment at the recent output of the Rump. John Lilburne and the other Leveller leaders had been committed to the Tower in March 1649 for their publication of the two-part *England's New Chains Discovered*. Earlier in their development, they had embellished their core programme for political and legal reform with a demand for enclosed land to be 'laid open againe to the free and common use'.[15] They became more circumspect, however, professing in April 1649 that 'we never had it in our thoughts to level mens estates, it being the utmost of our aime that the Commonwealth be reduced to such a passe that every man may with as much security as may be enjoy his propriety'.[16] Their third *Agreement of the People* repeated this assertion.[17] In June they explicitly rejected 'the erroneous tenets of the poor Diggers at George Hill'.[18] Winstanley's strategy of clinging to the coattails of Leveller popularity was shrewd enough, but the Levellers were a differently constituted movement: they 'represented the interests of people of some modest economic independence, small traders and craftsmen and the like, rather than those of the great mass of the poor'.[19] The Diggers set out to appeal 'to those whom the "constitutional" Levellers at Putney would not have enfranchised – servants, labourers, paupers, the economically unfree'.[20]

We will not understand the 'levelling' tendency in the English Revolution unless we keep in mind the phenomenon of enclosure, that epoch-making 'usurpation of the common lands' which had its origin in the fifteenth century.[21] 'Although the soil of the waste was vested in the manorial lord, his possession was qualified by the recognition in English common law of use-rights attaching to copyholds and freeholds within the manor.'[22] 'To enclose land was to extinguish common rights over it, thus putting an end to all common grazing.'[23] The business of hedging in land created space under the landowner's absolute control for sheep-walks or improved cultivation. Whereas larger tenants might be co-opted with favourable leases on enclosed waste, 'smallholders, landless cottagers and rural artisans were inadequately compensated for their loss of access to the commons and wastes, or not at all, and lost their cushion against dependence on wage labour'.[24] It was the end of the traditional nexus of rights and obligations in the countryside; lords of manors and their farmers were winding down feudalism on their own terms. Evictions, depopulation, competitive rents, pauperism and a tradition of rural protest were among the results. A sizeable anti-enclosure uprising in the Midlands in 1607 generated the epithets of 'Digger' and

'Leveller'. The 1640s saw direct action in numerous counties as both landlord and landless took advantage of the social disarray. Keith Thomas contends that 'the whole Digger movement can be plausibly regarded as the culmination of a century of unauthorized encroachment upon the forests and wastes by squatters and local commoners, pushed on by land shortage and the pressure of population'.[25] The situation was less acute in Walton, where unenclosed land was plentiful and manorial control 'relatively lax'. In Cobham, on the other hand, there had been 'protracted landlord–tenant conflict' over increased exactions on copyhold tenants.[26]

In the aftermath of the war, high taxation, dreadful harvests and soaring bread prices brought immense hardship. Fellow Diggers in a commune that appeared in Wellingborough, Northamptonshire, described how in their parish alone over one thousand people were dependent on alms. 'We have spent all we have,' they explained, 'our trading is decayed, our wives and children cry for bread, our lives are a burden to us, divers of us having 5. 6. 7. 8. 9. in Family, and we cannot get bread for one of them by our labor.'[27] Victory in the war had brought into Parliament's possession crown land and royalist estates. Winstanley was not alone in urging a redistribution of the spoils to ease the distress of the poor; a group of Buckinghamshire polemicists, alternately categorized as radical Levellers or near-Diggers, had issued a similar call in December 1648.[28] The disposal of seized land had a direct application to the commune on St George's Hill: Walton was a crown manor leased to the courtier Drake family. The Diggers submitted to Fairfax when he visited on 30 May 1649 that 'the King that possest [the lands] by the Norman Conquest being dead, they were returned againe to the Common people'.[29] It would set a mighty precedent if they could make that assertion stand.

The king's defeat had tremendous repercussions in Digger

minds. The Diggers not only conflated the standard parlia-
mentarian account of 'Norman' tyranny with Biblical history
– conjuring up in Stuart England the 'Babylonish yoke laid
upon Israel of old'; they also surpassed commonplace appeals
to lost Anglo-Saxon liberties by stressing the feudal property
relations instigated by the Conqueror.[30] If the death of William
of Normandy's 'descendant', Charles I, was truly to terminate
a centuries-old tyranny, then private property itself would have
to go. While property lasted, so too would the baleful Norman
legacy. Winstanley commented that as a result of the regicide,
'that top-bow is lopped off the tree of Tyrannie, and Kingly
power in that one particular is cast out'. However, 'oppression
is a great tree still, and keeps off the son of freedome from the
poor Commons still'.[31]

In Winstanley's view the Roundhead leaders had yet to
deliver on their wartime contract with the people. *A Declaration
from the Poor oppressed People of England*, the second Digger
manifesto, published by 1 June 1649, outlined this premise:
'the Parliament promised, if we would pay taxes, and give
free quarter, and adventure our lives against *Charles* and his
party... they would make us a free people'. It had not come to
pass. The Diggers had already elaborated in *The True Levellers
Standard Advanced* that freedom for them meant access to the
land, direct production in place of wage labour. '*England* is
not a Free people,' they averred, 'till the Poor that have no
Land, have a free allowance to dig and labour the Commons,
and so live as Comfortably as the Landlords that live in their
Inclosures.'

What were the implications of the Digger plan for parallel
property systems – communism for the poor and private ownership among the rich? *A Letter to The Lord Fairfax*, delivered to
the Lord General on 9 June, gave notice of the Diggers' intent
to withdraw from the jurisdiction of the Commonwealth:

> while we keep within the bounds of our Commons, and
> none of us shall be found guilty of medling with your goods,
> or inclosed proprieties, unlesse the Spirit in you freely give
> it up, your laws then shall not reach to us, unlesse you will
> oppresse or shed the blood of the innocent.

The attempt to escape both universal church and magistracy was typical of Anabaptists and other sectaries. Winstanley differed by declaring off-limits from civil authority not a religious community per se, but the inhabitants of an archipelago of common lands. He grandiosely laid claim on behalf of the people to 'all the Commons and waste Ground in *England*, and in the whole World'.[32] The Diggers planned to raise a stock to fund their future growth by monopolizing the then very lucrative trade in timber. 'What seems to have been envisaged ... was the creation of a national movement of Digger communities, which they hoped would have sufficient staying power to continue from one generation to the next.'[33] It was not immediately obvious that their target recruits – cottagers, labourers and the like – would automatically welcome the loss of rough pasture to Digger cultivation.[34]

Official reaction to the Diggers was swift but mercifully uncoordinated. The Council of State was quickly apprised by a Walton yeoman that the Diggers 'threaten to pull downe and levell all parke pales' and 'give out they will bee four or five thousand within 10 days'.[35] Other accounts alleged that they would soon spread to Hampstead, Hounslow and Newmarket heaths and thereby encircle the capital.[36] The Council thought the Diggers 'ridiculous' but feared that 'greater mischief' might arise. It therefore recommended to Fairfax that cavalry be sent to disperse the mob. Only the disinterested attitude of the Lord General's envoy – 'the business is not worth the writing nor yet taking notiss of' – won the Diggers a reprieve.[37] They also expressed gratitude for the 'mildnesse and moderation' of the Lord General himself.[38] Winstanley believed he had reached an understanding with the military authorities: 'that you would not meddle with us, but leave us to the Law of the Land, and the Country Gentlemen to deal with us'.[39]

This left enemies enough for the Diggers to contend with. Their subsequent pamphlets describe the violence meted out by Walton freeholders and farmers together with – to Winstanley's dismay – some of the local soldiery and lower orders. 'The most intense local opposition to the Diggers came from those Walton residents who lived near St George's Hill, and who had most to lose from incursions on that part of the heath.'[40] Winstanley and several other colonists were dragged through the courts for trespass. Sometime in August 1649 they opted to relocate to Cobham, where a lot of them had family connections and residences. There the attacks continued, orchestrated by the lord of the manor, John Platt. 'In Cobham, much more so than in Walton, the impetus for attacks on the Diggers seems to have come from landowners anxious to protect manorial resources to which they claimed title.'[41] Winstanley relates the many instances when Platt's thugs attacked men, women and children, pulled down Digger houses, destroyed their tools and trampled their crops. By early 1650 the Diggers were 'like to flagge and droppe'. They sent out messengers to seek aid from friends and sympathizers. *A Letter Taken at Wellinborough* gives their itinerary. The couriers helped to initiate and consolidate a network of Digger colonies in and around the Home Counties – in Barnet, Enfield, Dunstable, Iver in Buckinghamshire, unknown places in Gloucestershire, Kent and Nottinghamshire, and the aforementioned Wellingborough. 'Digger influence spread all over southern and central England', comments Christopher Hill.[42] But it did so ephemerally. Platt brutally dispersed the Cobham Diggers on 19 April, barely a year after they had come together on St George's Hill. His men kept lookout on the heath to prevent their return. Soon the other Digger settlements disappeared. As Winstanley had foreseen in *A New-yeers Gift for the Parliament and Armie*:

[H]ere I end, having put my Arm as far as my strength will
go to advance Righteousness: I have Writ, I have Acted, I
have Peace: and now I must wait to see the Spirit do his own
work in the hearts of others, and whether *England* shall be
the first Land, or some others, wherein Truth shall sit down
in triumph.

After a period of drift, Winstanley wrote his last work, *The Law
of Freedom in a Platform*, in 1651, published the following year.
The book delegated to Cromwell, by then commander-in-chief
of the army, the task of 'set[ting] the Land free to the oppressed
Commoners'.[43] The magistrate, hitherto marginalized, was now
the centrepiece of his much revised utopia. This was a significant
change in approach, dictated by hard circumstance. However,
Winstanley had always entertained the view that the republic
might actually deliver on its reforming potential, hence his appeals
to its leading figures. He enthusiastically took the Engagement to
be 'true and faithful to the Commonwealth' in March 1650. It
was not the conduct of any ordinary religious separatist. G. E.
Aylmer argues Winstanley 'was surely correct to suppose that the
maintenance of republican rule was a necessary precondition for
further economic and social change'.[44] But could the landowners assembled in Parliament be expected to move in an egalitar-
ian direction? Winstanley himself noted the 'partiality' or double
standards in which they indulged, securing their own land through
the abolition of feudal wardship while doing nothing to protect
tenants.[45] In 1648 these same landowners had preferred the army
to purge their ranks than face a dissolution and fresh elections.
They declined to tackle either enclosures or tithes, and they were
shortly to crown Cromwell as Lord Protector. The restoration of
Charles II when it came in 1660 was not their sole compromise.

The great wave of Civil War religious radicalism ultimately
subsided into Quaker quietism and respectable non-conformity.
The Diggers lay largely forgotten in the archives until the late

nineteenth century, when C. H. Firth's second volume of the
Clarke Papers brought to light official documents pertaining to
them and even a transcript of the 'Digger song'. Winstanley
was soon adopted by Quakers seeking ancestors; Quaker scholar
Lewis Berens published a book-length study in 1906.[46] In the
Soviet era, David Petegorsky's more systematic *Left-Wing
Democracy in the English Civil War* – a product of interwar doctoral
research under Harold Laski at the London School of Economics
– was followed by two separate projects at Cornell and Oxford
to publish Winstanley's writings.[47] Neither in fact produced a
full set, which would only arrive through a transatlantic col-
laboration in 2009.[48] The long interval between these publish-
ing milestones belonged to radical Oxford historian Christopher
Hill. Hill contributed an introduction to Hamilton's 1944 collection. The new edition of Winstanley's complete works is
dedicated to Hill's memory. Hill published his own selection
in 1973.[49] His tutorials were the acknowledged inspiration for
David Caute's historical novel *Comrade Jacob* (1961), which
served as the basis for Kevin Brownlow and Andrew Mollo's
1975 film *Winstanley*. Archival work has resolved some of the
uncertainties surrounding Winstanley's biography and the chro-
nology of Digger tracts, and also unearthed the odd forgotten
text.[50] John Gurney's recent *Brave Community* provides a micro-
scopic analysis of seventeenth-century Cobham. This activity
should not, however, be taken to imply that the Diggers have
entered the academic mainstream. In standard accounts of the
period they still attract very little attention. Austin Woolrych's
important *Britain in Revolution* devotes only a couple of pages to
this 'ripple' on the history of the Commonwealth.[51]

Hill maintained that 'the Diggers have something to say to
twentieth-century socialists'.[52] What can we conclude today?
The world has not moved any closer to Winstanley's ideals;
quite the reverse. On 29 October 2010 the Cameron government announced plans to sell off vast swathes of Britain's

748,000 hectares of publicly owned woodland to developers, in the biggest sale of public land for decades. According to Defra, registered common land now accounts for three per cent of England's total land area. A reclamation is overdue.

NOTES

1 Quoted in G. M. Trevelyan, *History of England* (3rd ed., London 1952), p. 420. S. R. Gardiner, in contrast, renders it: 'No one *rises so high* as he who knows not whither he is going' [emphasis added]. Gardiner, *Oliver Cromwell* (London 1909), p. 103.

2 See Brian Manning, *1649: The Crisis of the English Revolution* (London 1992).

3 Bulstrode Whitelocke, *Memorials of the English Affairs* (Oxford 1853), vol. 3, p. 18.

4 John Gurney, *Brave Community: The Digger Movement in the English Revolution* (Manchester 2007), pp. 131–4.

5 Gurney, *Brave Community*, p. 77. See also the biographical appendix to Thomas N. Corns, Ann Hughes and David Loewenstein (eds), *The Complete Works of Gerrard Winstanley*, vol. 2 (Oxford 2009), pp. 446–7.

6 Corns, et al., *Complete Works*, vol. 1, p. 4.

7 See *A Watch-Word to The City of London*.

8 Corns, et al., *Complete Works*, vol. 1, p. 23.

9 *Truth Lifting Up Its Head above Scandals* (1648), in Corns, et al., *Complete Works*, vol. 1, p. 449.

10 See *A Watch-Word to The City of London*.

11 David Cressy, *England on Edge: Crisis and Revolution 1640–1642* (Oxford 2006), p. 219.

12 David W. Petegorsky, *Left-Wing Democracy in the English Civil War* (London [1940] 1999), p. 126; Lewis H. Berens, *The Digger Movement in the Days of the Commonwealth* (Monmouth 2007), p. 71.

13 Corns, et al., *Complete Works*, vol. 1, pp. 472–568.

14 For the Levellers see Geoffrey Robertson's introduction to the Verso companion volume, *The Levellers: The Putney Debates* (London 2007).

15 Richard Overton, *An Appeale*, in Don M. Wolfe (ed.), *Leveller Manifestoes of the Puritan Revolution* (New York 1967), p. 194.

16 *A Manifestation*, in Wolfe, *Leveller Manifestoes*, p. 391.

17 *An Agreement of the Free People of England*, in Wolfe, *Leveller Manifestoes*, p. 409.

18 Petegorsky, *Left-Wing Democracy*, p. 162n.

19 Austin Woolrych, *Britain in Revolution* (Oxford 2009), pp. 389–90.

20 Christopher Hill (ed.), *Winstanley: The Law of Freedom and Other Writings* (Cambridge 1983), p. 30.

21 Karl Marx, *Capital*, vol. 1, trans. by Ben Fowkes (London 1990), p. 878.

22 Roger B. Manning, *Village Revolts: Social Protest and Popular Disturbances in England, 1509–1640* (Oxford 1988), p. 19.

23 Joan Thirsk, 'Enclosing and Engrossing', in Thirsk (ed.), *The Agrarian History of England and Wales*, (Cambridge 1967), vol. 4, p. 200.

24 Brian Manning, *The Far Left in the English Revolution* (London 1999), pp. 23–4.

25 Keith Thomas, 'Another Digger Broadside', *Past and Present*, 42 (February 1969), p. 58.

26 Gurney, *Brave Community*, pp. 16–20, 138 and 155.

27 Gurney, *Brave Community*, p. 188.

28 Gurney, *Brave Community*, p. 111.

29 Gurney, *Brave Community*, p. 139.

30 On the Norman Yoke see Christopher Hill, *Puritanism and Revolution: Studies in Interpretation of the English Revolution of the Seventeenth Century* (London 1958).

31 See *A New-yeers Gift for the Parliament and Armie*.

32 See *The True Levellers Standard Advanced*.

33 Gurney, *Brave Community*, p. 142.

34 Manning, *1649*, p. 131.

35 C. H. Firth (ed.), *The Clarke Papers: Selections from the Papers of William Clarke, Secretary to the Council of the Army, 1647–1649, and to General Monck and the Commanders of the Army in Scotland, 1651–1660* (London 1894), vol. 2, pp. 209–11.

36 Gurney, *Brave Community*, p. 141.

37 Firth (ed.), *The Clarke Papers*, p. 212.

38 See *A Letter to The Lord Fairfax*. The *Declaration from Sir Thomas Fairfax and the Army* of June 1647 had included a demand, so dear to the Diggers, for liberty of conscience.

39 See *A New-yeers Gift for the Parliament and Armie*.

40 Gurney, *Brave Community*, p. 155.

41 Gurney, *Brave Community*, p. 169.

42 Christopher Hill, *The World Turned Upside Down* (London 1991), p. 128.

43 'I have set the candle at your door', says Winstanley, 'for you have power in your hand . . . to Act for Common Freedom if you will; I have no power.' Corns, et al., *Complete Works*, vol. 2, pp. 279 and 288.

44 G. E. Aylmer, 'England's Spirit Unfoulded, Or an Incouragement to Take the *Engagement*: A Newly Discovered Pamphlet by Gerrard Winstanley', *Past and Present* 40 (July 1968), p. 6.

45 See below, p. 136, n8 and n9.

46 Berens is candid enough to describe one of Winstanley's early tracts as 'long, wearisome and almost unreadable'. He also spares the reader most of the Diggers' attempts at verse. Berens, *The Digger Movement*, pp. 56 and 152.

47 Petegorsky, *Left-Wing Democracy in the English Civil War* (London [1940] 1999); George H. Sabine (ed.), *The Works of Gerrard Winstanley* (Ithaca NY, 1941), Leonard Hamilton (ed.), *Gerrard Winstanley: Selections from his works* (London 1944).

48 Thomas N. Corns, Ann Hughes and David Loewenstein (eds), *The Complete Works of Gerrard Winstanley*, (Oxford 2009) two vols. The editors are based at the universities of Bangor, Keele and Wisconsin–Madison.

49 Hill argues that Winstanley had arrived at 'a crucial point in modern political thinking: that state power is related to the property system and to the body of ideas which supports that system'. Hill (ed.), *Winstanley: The Law of Freedom*, p. 9.

50 See G. E. Aylmer, 'England's Spirit Unfoulded', and Keith Thomas' two articles in *Past and Present* 42 (February 1969): 'Another Digger Broadside', pp. 57–68; and 'The Date of Gerrard Winstanley's *Fire in the Bush*', pp. 160–2.

51 Woolrych, *Britain in Revolution*, pp. 449–50.

52 Hill, *The World Turned Upside Down*, p. 15.

Introduction

by Tony Benn

Not everyone realizes that we had a revolution in England long before the French Revolution, the American Revolution or the Russian Revolution. The legacy it has left for us is of supreme relevance today.

The overthrow and execution of the king, after a civil war that was led by parliament against the monarchy, began a long period of change and ended with the return of the monarchy and the beginning of what we call parliamentary democracy. But during those troubled years things were said that are as true today as they were at the time, and arguments were put forward that would still arouse the same controversy.

So stimulating were these ideas that the Agreement of the People came to the attention of some revolutionary Frenchmen in Bordeaux, who translated it into French and established a revolutionary centre in Bordeaux, which no doubt played some part in formulating the ideas which emerged in 1789.

The Agreement of the People was an early democratic statement, and in it we find ideas which are just as relevant as they were at the time. And indeed played some part in the drafting of the American constitution. Kings and political leaders are remembered for the ideas they imposed on those they governed, but all real progress comes from ideas that begin at the bottom and force their way to the top. For example, the demand that women be given the right to vote was first ignored by the powerful. When the campaign grew, it was denounced as dangerous and the suffragettes were imprisoned, some went on hunger strike and were forcibly fed by wardresses. Then when the argument had been won you could not find anyone in power who didn't seem to be claiming that they thought of the idea in the first place.

The early seventeenth century launched into the public domain arguments about freedom and equality and democracy which we would now all regard as normal – even though at the time they were considered totally destructive of the status quo. The conflict between the king and parliament was about power, and it released a wider argument about democracy, which is what the Levellers were about. But it was the True Levellers who really carried the case forward to a deep philosophical level and decided to do something about it by digging on land they believed to be common.

The Diggers, as they were also known, were the first true socialists, and Winstanley was their spokesman who wrote deeply thoughtful statements of the case for the common ownership of land, linking his ideas to the Norman Conquest, which as he pointed out was all about who controlled the land.

I find there is one speech Winstanley allegedly delivered on 1 May 1649 which sets out the whole case in language that is unforgettable. In the beginning of time, said Winstanley,

the great Creator Reason, made the Earth to be a Common Treasury, to preserve Beasts, Birds, Fishes, and Man, the lord that was to govern this Creation; for Man had Domination given to him, over the Beasts, Birds and Fishes; but not one word was spoken in the beginning, That one branch of mankind should rule over another.

And the Reason is this, Every single man, Male and Female, is a perfect Creature of himself; and the same Spirit that made the Globe, dwels in man to govern the Globe; so that the flesh of man being subject to reason, his Maker, hath him to be his Teacher and Ruler within himself, therefore needs not run abroad after any Teacher and Ruler without him, for he needs not that any man should teach him, for the same Anoynting that ruled in the Son of man, teacheth him all things.

In that passage is contained some of the most important radical ideas of all time, from the belief that the earth was created by reason to the recognition of sexist language and the belief that we are all able to reach our own judgement in the light of what we have brought to the world. It also makes clear that "the earth is a common treasury" and centres the ownership of land at the heart of politics.

These words have the power to move people and give them confidence in their own ability to think things out for themselves, which offers encouragement to those who might otherwise be tempted to believe that the problems are so great nothing can be done about them.

The English revolution did not produce what its sponsors dreamed of, but it left us this language and these ideas to think over again and to see what they have to offer us now. That is the debt we offer to those who fought so hard to win our rights nearly four hundred years ago, and this book, which is long overdue, offers us a text for our study of the key issues in the politics of tomorrow.

Suggested Further Reading

COLLECTED WORKS:

The Complete Works of Gerrard Winstanley, ed. Thomas N. Corns, Ann
Hughes, David Loewenstein (Oxford: Oxford University Press, 2010)
Winstanley: 'The Law of Freedom' and other writings, ed. Christopher Hill
(Cambridge: Cambridge University Press, 1973).

SECONDARY SOURCES:

Aylmer, G. E., 'The Religion of Gerrard Winstanley' in *Radical
Religion in the English Revolution*, ed. J. F. McGregor and B. Reay
(Oxford: Oxford University Press, 1988).
Berens, L. H., *The Digger Movement in the Days of the Commonwealth*
(London: Simpkin, Marshall, Hamilton, Kent & Co. Ltd., 1906).
Bernstein, Eduard, *Cromwell and Communism* (London: Allen &
Unwin, 1930).
Gurney, John, *Brave Community: The Digger Movement in the English
Revolution* (Manchester: Manchester University Press, 2007).
Hill, Christopher, *The World Turned Upside Down* (Harmondsworth:
Penguin Books, 1978).
Holstun, James, *Ehud's Dagger: Class Struggle in the English Revolution*
(London: Verso, 2002).

Hopton, Andrew, ed., *Digger Tracts 1649–50* (London: Aporia Press, 1989).

Manning, Brian, *1649: The Crisis of the English Revolution* (London: Bookmarks, 1992).

Morton, A. L., *The World of the Ranters: Religious Radicalism in the English Revolution* (London: Lawrence & Wishart, 1970).

Petegorsky, David W., *Left-Wing Democracy in the English Civil War* (London: Victor Gollancz, 1940).

Zagorin, Perez, *A History of Political Thought in the English Revolution* (London: Routledge & Kegan Paul, 1954).

A Note on the Texts

Andrew Hopton

This selection focusses on works from the period of 1649–50 during which the Digger colony in Surrey (of which Winstanley was the chief spokesman) flourished and eventually collapsed after repeated harassment by the local authorities. The texts included are arranged chronologically. They are *The True Levellers Standard Advanced* and *A Declaration from the Poor oppressed people of England*, the first two publications issued by the Digger colony; a letter in which Winstanley puts forward the Diggers' case to Lord Fairfax (General of the English Forces) and other members of the victorious army council (*A Letter to The Lord Fairfax*); two pamphlets which give details of the treatment of the Diggers at the hands of the local authorities and which also advance the Digger programme (*A Watch-Word to The City of London, and the Armie* and *A New-yeers Gift for the Parliament and Armie*); *A Vindication of Those ... called Diggers*, a pamphlet in which Winstanley attacks Ranters and dissociates the Diggers from Ranterism; the penultimate Surrey Digger tract, *An Appeale to all Englishmen*, reiterating the Digger position in the face of increasing opposition; and finally, a letter taken by the authorities from Digger emissaries who had travelled the countryside to promote the Digger cause, on their arrest at Wellingborough, the site of another colony (cf. *Digger Tracts 1649–50*, Aporia Press, 1989).

The works reproduced in this edition follow as faithfully as possible the original publications. A few alterations have been made in the case of very obvious typographical errors. Otherwise the (often idiosyncratic) spelling and punctuation of the original works have been preserved throughout. The layout of the original pamphlets has also been followed, though rationalized to fit the format of the present edition. In all instances the aim has been to make the texts as accurate and readable as possible.

The texts are all taken from originals in the British Library's Thomason collection.

The True

Levellers Standard
ADVANCED:

OR,

**The State of Community opened, and Presented to the
Sons of Men.**

By

	Ferrard Winstanley,
William Everard,	*Richard Goodgroome,*
Iohn Palmer,	*Thomas Starre,*
Iohn South,	*William Hoggrill,*
Iohn Courton.	*Robert Sawyer,*
William Taylor,	*Thomas Eder,*
Christopher Clifford,	*Henry Bickerstaffe,*
Iohn Barker.	*Iohn Taylor,* &c.

**Beginning to Plant and Manure the Waste land upon
George-Hill, in the Parish of *Walton*, in the
County of *Surrey*.**[1]

LONDON,
Printed in the Yeer, MDCXLIX.

TO ALL MY FELLOW CREATURES THAT
SHALL VIEW THESE ENSUING LINES

The God of this world blinding the eyes of the men of the world, have taken possession of them and their Lives, Rules and Raigns, and in a high measure opposeth the everlasting spirit, the King of Righteousness; both in them, and on the whole Creation, bending all its wit and power to destroy this spirit, and the persons in whom it lives, rules and governs; making Lawes under specious pretences, yea and penalties too, that all Nations, Tongues, and Languages, shall fall down and worship this god, become subject, yea in slavery to it, and to the men in whom it dwels: But the god of this world is Pride and Covetousness, the rootes of all Evil, from whence flowes all the wickedness that is acted under the Sun, as Malice, Tyranny, Lording over, and despising their fellow Creatures, killing and destroying those that will not, or cannot become subject to their Tyranny, to uphold their Lordly Power, Pride, and Covetousness.

I have had some Conversation with the Author of this ensuing Declaration, and the Persons Subscribing, and by experience find them sweetly acted and guided by the everlasting spirit, the Prince of Peace, to walk in the paths of Righteousness, not daring to venture upon any acts of injustice, but endeavouring to do unto all, as they would have done to them, *having Peace and Joy in themselves, knit together and united in one Spirit of Glory and Truth, Love to their fellow Creatures, Contentation*[2] *with Food and Rayment, shewing much Humility and Meekness of spirit; such as these shall be partakers of the Promise.*

Blessed are the Meek, for they shall inherit the Earth.

Secondly, For this action of theirs, in labouring to Manure the wast places of the Earth, it is an action full of Iustice and Righteousnesse, full of Love and Charity to their fellow Creatures; nothing of the god of this world, Pride and Covetousnesse seen in it, no self-seeking, or glorifying in the Flesh.

Vouchsafe to reade, or view over these ensuing Lines yee Powers of the Earth; Oh that Reason might sit upon the throne of your hearts as Iudge; I am confident there is nothing written in anger or hatred to your persons, but in love to them as fellow Creatures; but against that which have bound up your own Spirits in slavery; if you could speak impartially, your own Consciences can bear me witnesse, and only bears sway in your forcing you to exercise Tyranny, scourging and trampling under foot your fellow Creatures, especially those whose eyes are opened and can cleerly discover the great Devil, Tyranny, Pride, and Covetousnesse working to and fro upon your Spirits, and raigning in you, which will prove your own destruction: The Angels that kept not their first Estate, are reserved under Chains of darknesse unto the Iudgment of the great day.

The whole Creation are the Angels of the everlasting Spirit of Righteousnesse, they are all ministring spirits, speaking every Creature in its kind the Will of the Father. The Chariots of God are 20000 thousands of Angels, *Psal. &c.*

But yee the great ones of the Earth, the Powers of this world, yee are the Angels that kept not your first estate, and now remain under Chains of darknesse: Your first Estate was Innocency and Equallity with your fellow Creatures, but your Lordly power over them, both Persons and Consciences, your proud fleshly imaginations, lofty thoughts of your selves, are the fruits of darknesse which you are kept under: The whole Creation groaneth and is in bondage, even until now, waiting for deliverance, and must wait till he that with-holdeth be taken away, the man of sin, that Antichrist which sits in the throne, in the hearts of the men of this world, the Powers of the Earth, above all that is called God.

I know you have high thoughts of your selves, think you know much, and see much, but the Light that is in you is Darknesse; and how great is that darknesse? They that live in the light of the Spirit can discover that to be the blacknesse of darknesse which you count light. And truly, a great Light, a bright Morning Star which will flourish and spread it self, shining in Darknesse, and darknesse shall not be able to comprehend it, though you Spurn never so much against it.

I expect nothing but opposition, mockings, deridings from Lord Esau *the man of Flesh: I know it will be counted in the eye of Flesh, a foolish undertaking, an object of scorn and laughter; but in this is their Comfort and incouragement, That the power of Life and Light, the Spirit by whom they are commanded, will carry them on, strengthen and support them, rescuing them from the Jaw of the Lyon and Paw of the Bear; For great is the work which will shortly be done upon the Earth. Despise not Visions, Voyces and Revelations; examine the Scriptures, Prophesies are now fulfilling; be not like* Josephs *Brethren, speak not evil of things you know not: For whatsoever is of God will stand, do what you can, though you may crush it for a time, the time is neer expired it will spring up again and flourish like a green Bay tree: What is not of the Father will fall to the ground, though you bend all your wit, power and policy to keep it up; but of that will be no Resurrection. That the eternal Spirit may enlighten you, that Reason may dwel in you, and act accordingly, is the desire of your Loving Friend, and Fellow Creature,*

April 20,
1649.   **JOHN TAYLOR.**[3]

A Declaration to the Powers of England, *and to all the Powers of the World, shewing the Cause why the Common People of* England *have begun, and gives Consent to Digge up, Manure, and Sow Corn upon* George-Hill *in* Surrey; *by those that have Subscribed, and thousands more that gives Consent.*

In the beginning of Time, the great Creator Reason, made the Earth to be a Common Treasury, to preserve Beasts, Birds, Fishes, and Man, the lord that was to govern this Creation; for Man had Domination given to him, over the Beasts, Birds, and Fishes; but not one word was spoken in the beginning, That one branch of mankind should rule over another.

And the Reason is this, Every single man, Male and Female, is a perfect Creature of himself; and the same Spirit that made the Globe, dwels in man to govern the Globe; so that the flesh of man being subject to Reason, his Maker, hath him to be his Teacher and Ruler within himself, therefore needs not run abroad after any Teacher and Ruler without him, for he needs not that any man should teach him, for the same Anoynting that ruled in the Son of man, teacheth him all things.

But since humane flesh (that king of Beasts) began to delight himself in the objects of the Creation, more then in the Spirit Reason and Righteousness, who manifests himself to be the indweller in the Five Sences, of Hearing, Seeing, Tasting, Smelling, Feeling; then he fell into blindness of mind and weakness of heart, and runs abroad for a Teacher and Ruler: And so selfish imaginations taking possession of the Five Sences, and ruling as King in the room of Reason therein, and working with Covetousnesse, did set up one man to teach and rule over another; and thereby the Spirit was killed, and man was brought into bondage, and became a greater Slave to such of his own kind, then the Beasts of the field were to him.

And hereupon, The Earth (which was made to be a Common Treasury of relief for all, both Beasts and Men) was hedged in to In-closures[4] by the teachers and rulers, and the others were made Servants and Slaves: And that Earth that is within this Creation made a Common Store-house for all, is bought and sold, and kept in the hands of a few, whereby the great Creator is mightily dishonored, as if he were a respector of persons, delighting in the comfortable Livelihood of some, and rejoycing in the miserable povertie and straits of others. From the beginning it was not so.

But this coming in of Bondage, is called *A-dam*, because this ruling and teaching power without, doth *dam* up the Spirit of Peace and Liberty; First within the heart, by filling it with slavish fears of others. Secondly without, by giving the bodies of one to be imprisoned, punished and oppressed by the outward power of another. And this evil was brought upon us through his own Covetousnesse, whereby he is blinded and made weak, and sees not the Law of Righteousnesse in his heart, which is the pure light of Reason, but looks abroad for it, and thereby the Creation is cast under bondage and curse, and the creator is sleighted; First by the Teachers and Rulers that sets themselves down in the Spirits room, to teach and rule, where he himself is only King. Secondly by the other, that refuses the Spirit, to be taught and governed by fellow Creatures, and this was called Israels Sin, in casting off the Lord and chusing *Saul*, one like themselves to be their King, when as they had the same Spirit of Reason and government in themselves, as he had, if they were but subject. And Israels rejecting of outward teachers and rulers to embrace the Lord, and to be all taught and ruled by that righteous King, that *Jeremiah* Prophesied shall rule in the new Heavens and new Earth in the latter dayes, will be their Restauration from bondage, *Ier.* 23.5,6.

But for the present state of the old World that is running up like parchment in the fire, and wearing away, we see proud Imaginary flesh, which is the wise Serpent, rises up in flesh and gets dominion is some to rule over others, and so forces one part of the Creation man, to be a slave to another; and thereby the Spirit is killed in both. The one looks upon himself as a teacher and ruler, and so is lifted up in pride over his fellow Creature: The other looks upon himself as imperfect, and so is dejected in his Spirit, and looks upon his fellow Creature of his own Image, as a Lord above him.

And thus *Esau*, the man of flesh, which is Covetousness and Pride, hath killed *Jacob*, the Spirit of meeknesse, and righteous government in the light of Reason, and rules over him: And so the Earth that was made a common Treasury for all to live comfortably upon, is become through mans unrighteous actions one over another, to be a place, wherein one torments another.

Now the great Creator, who is the Spirit Reason, suffered himself thus to be rejected, and troden underfoot by the covetous proud flesh, for a certain time limited; therefore saith he, *The Seed out of whom the Creation did proceed, which is my Self, shall bruise this Serpents head, and restore my Creation again from this curse and bondage; and when I the King of Righteousnesse raigns in every man, I will be the blessing of the Earth, and the joy of all Nations.*

And since the coming in of the stoppage, or the *A-dam* the Earth hath been inclosed and given to the Elder brother *Esau*, or man of flesh, and hath been bought and sold from one to another; and *Iacob*, or the younger brother, that is to succeed or come forth next, who is the universal spreading power of righteousnesse that gives liberty to the whole Creation, is made a servant.

And this Elder Son, or man of bondage, hath held the Earth in bondage to himself, not by a meek Law of Righteousnesse, But by subtle selfish Councels, and by open and violent force; for wherefore is it that there is such Wars and rumours of Wars in the Nations of the Earth? and wherefore are men so mad to destroy one another? But only to uphold Civil propriety of Honor, Dominion and Riches one over another, which is the curse the Creation groans under, waiting for deliverance.

But when once the Earth becomes a Common Treasury again, as it must, for all the Prophesies of Scriptures and Reason are Circled here in this Community, and mankind must have the Law of Righteousnesse once more writ in his heart, and all must be made of one heart, and one mind.

Then this Enmity in all Lands will cease, for none shall dare to seek a Dominion over others, neither shall any dare to kill another, nor desire more of the Earth then another; for he that will rule over, imprison, oppresse, and kill his fellow Creatures, under what pretence soever, is a destroyer of the Creation, and an actor of the Curse, and walks contrary to the rule of right-eousnesse: (*Do, as you would have others do to you; and love your Enemies, not in words, but in actions*).

Therefore you powers of the Earth, or Lord *Esau*, the Elder brother, because you have appeared to rule the Creation, first take notice, That the power that sets you to work, is selvish Covetousness, and an aspiring Pride, to live in glory and ease over *Iacob*, the meek Spirit; that is, the Seed that lies hid, in & among the poor Common People, or younger Brother, out of whom the blessing of Deliverance is to rise and spring up to all Nations.

And Reason, the living king of righteousnesse, doth only look on, and lets thee alone, That whereas thou counts thy self an Angel of Light, thou shalt appear in the light of the Sun, to be a Devil, *A-dam*, and the Curse that the Creation groans under; and the time is now come for thy downfal, and *Iacob* must rise, who is the universal Spirit of love and righteousnesse, that fils, and will fill all the Earth.

Thou teaching and ruling power of flesh, thou hast had three periods of time, to vaunt thy self over thy Brother; the first was from the time of thy coming in, called *A-dam*, or a stoppage, till *Moses* came; and there thou that wast a self-lover in *Cain*, killed thy brother *Abel*, a plain-hearted man that loved righteousnesse: And thou by thy wisdom and beastly government, made the whole Earth to stinck, till *Noah* came, which was a time of the world, like the coming in of the watery Seed into the womb, towards the bringing forth of the man child.

And from *Noah* till Moses came, thou still hast ruled in vaunting, pride, and cruel oppression; *Ishmael* against *Isaac*, *Esau* against *Iacob*; for thou hast still been the man of flesh that hath ever persecuted the man of righteousnesse, the Spirit Reason.

And Secondly, from *Moses* till the *Son of Man* came, which was a time of the world, that the man child could not speak like a man, but lisping, making signs to shew his meaning; as we see many Creatures that cannot speak do. For *Moses* Law was a Language lapped up in Types, Sacrifices, Forms, and Customs, which was a weak time. And in this time likewise, O thou teaching and ruling power, thou wast an oppressor; for look into Scriptures and see if *Aaron* and the Priests were not the first that deceived the people; and the Rulers, as Kings and Governors, were continually the Ocean-head, out of whose power, Burdens, Oppressions, and Poverty did flow out upon the Earth: and these two Powers still hath been the Curse, that hath led the Earth, mankind, into confusion and death by their imaginary and selvish teaching and ruling, and it could be no otherwise; for while man looks upon himself, as an imperfect Creation, and seeks and runs abroad for a teacher and a ruler, he is all this time a stranger to the Spirit that is within himself.

But though the Earth hath been generally thus in darknesse, since the *A-dam* rise up, and hath owned a Light, and a Law without them to walk by, yet some have been found as watchmen, in this night time of the world, that have been taught by the Spirit within them, and not by any flesh without them, as *Abraham*, *Isaac*, *Iacob*, and the Prophets: And these, and such as these, have still been the Butt, at whom, the powers of the Earth in all ages of the world, by their selvish Laws, have shot their fury.

And then Thirdly, from the time of the *Son of man*, which was a time that the man-child began to speak like a child growing upward to manhood, till now, that the Spirit is rising up in strength. O thou teaching and ruling power of the earthy man, thou hast been an oppressor, by imprisonment, impoverishing, and martyrdom; and all thy power and wit, hath been to make Laws, and execute them against such as stand for universal Liberty, which is the rising up of *Iacob*; as by those ancient enslaving Laws not yet blotted out, but held up as weapons against the man-child.

O thou Powers of *England*, though thou hast promised to make this People a Free People,[5] yet thou hast so handled the matter, through thy self-seeking humour, That thou hast wrapped us up more in bondage, and oppression lies heavier upon us; not only bringing thy fellow Creatures, the Commoners, to a morsel of Bread, but by confounding all sorts of people by thy Government, of doing and undoing.

First, Thou hast made the people to take a Covenant and Oaths to endeavour a Reformation, and to bring in Liberty every man in his place; and yet while a man is in pursuing of that Covenant, he is imprisoned and oppressed by thy Officers, Courts, and Justices, so called.[6]

Thou hast made Ordinances to cast down Oppressing, Popish, Episcopal, Self-willed and Prerogative Laws;[7] yet we see, That Self-wil and Prerogative power, is the great standing Law, that rules all in action, and others in words.

Thou hast made many promises and protestations to make the Land a Free Nation: And yet at this very day, the same people, to whom thou hast made such Protestations of Liberty, are oppressed by thy Courts, Sizes,[8] Sessions, by thy Justices and Clarks of the Peace, so called, Bayliffs, Committees, are imprisoned, and forced to spend that bread, that should save their lives from Famine.

And all this, Because they stand to maintain an universal Liberty and Freedom, which not only is our Birthright, which our Maker gave us, but which thou hast promised to restore unto us, from under the former oppressing Powers that are gone before, and which likewise we have bought with our Money, in Taxes, Free-quarter,[9] and Bloud-shed; all which Sums thou hast received at our hands, and yet thou hast not given us our bargain.

O thou *A-dam*, thou *Esau*, thou *Cain*, thou Hypocritical man of flesh, when wilt thou cease to kill thy younger Brother? Surely thou must not do this great Work of advancing the Creation out of Bondage; for thou art lost extremely, and drowned in the Sea of Covetousnesse, Pride, and hardness of heart. *The blessing shall rise out of the dust which thou treadest under foot, Even the poor despised People, and they shall hold up Salvation to this Land, and to all Lands, and thou shalt be ashamed.*

Our Bodies as yet are in thy hand, our Spirit waits in quiet and peace, upon our Father for Deliverance; and if he give our Bloud into thy hand, for thee to spill, know this, That he is our Almighty Captain: And if some of you will not dare to shed your bloud, to maintain Tyranny and Oppression upon the Creation, know this, That our Bloud and Life shall not be unwilling to be delivered up in meekness to maintain universal Liberty, that so the Curse on our part may be taken off the Creation.

And we shall not do this by force of Arms, we abhorre it, For that is the work of the *Midianites*, to kill one another; But by obeying the Lord of Hosts, who hath Revealed himself in us, and to us, by labouring the Earth in righteousness together, to eat our bread with the sweat of our brows, neither giving hire, nor taking hire, but working together, and eating together, as one man, or as one house of Israel restored from Bondage; and so by the power of Reason, the Law of righteousness in us, we endeavour to lift up the Creation from that bondage of Civil Propriety, which it groans under.

We are made to hold forth this Declaration to you that are the Great Councel, and to you the Great Army of the Land of *England*,[10] that you may know what we would have, and what you are bound to give us by your Covenants and Promises; and that you may joyn with us in this Work, and so find Peace. Or else, if you do oppose us, we have peace in our Work, and in declaring this Report: And you shall be left without excuse.

The Work we are going about is this, To dig up *Georges-Hill* and the waste Ground thereabouts, and to Sow Corn, and to eat our bread together by the sweat of our brows.

And the First Reason is this, That we may work in righteousness, and lay the Foundation of making the Earth a Common Treasury for All, both Rich and Poor, That every one that is born in the Land, may be fed by the Earth his Mother that brought him forth, according to the Reason that rules in the Creation. Not Inclosing any part into any particular hand, but all as one man, working together, and feeding together as Sons of one Father, members of one Family; not one Lording over another, but all looking upon each other, as equals in the Creation; so that our Maker may be glorified in the work of his own hands, and that every one may see, he is no respecter of Persons, but equally loves his whole Creation, and hates nothing but the Serpent, which is Covetousness, branching forth into selvish Imagination, Pride, Envie, Hypocrisie, Uncleanness; all seeking the ease and honor of flesh, and fighting against the Spirit Reason that made the Creation; for that is the Corruption, the Curse, the Devil, the Father of Lies; Death and Bondage that Serpent and Dragon that the Creation is to be delivered from.

And we are moved hereunto for that Reason, and others which hath been shewed us, both by Vision, Voyce, and Revelation.

For it is shewed us, That so long as we, or any other, doth own the Earth to be the peculier Interest of Lords and Landlords, and not common to others as well as them, we own the Curse, and holds the Creation under bondage; and so long as we or any other doth own Landlords and Tennants, for one to call the Land his, or another to hire it of him, or for one to give hire, and for another to work for hire; this is to dishonour the work of Creation; as if the righteous Creator should have respect to persons, and therefore made the Earth for some, and not for all: And so long as we, or any other maintain this Civil Propriety, we consent still to hold the Creation down under that bondage it groans under, and so we should hinder the work of Restoration, and sin against Light that is given into us, and so through the fear of the flesh man, lose our peace.

And that this Civil Propriety is the Curse, is manifest thus, Those that Buy and Sell Land, and are landlords, have got it either by Oppression, or Murther, or Theft; and all landlords lives in the breach of the Seventh and Eighth Commandements, *Thou shalt not steal, nor kill.*

First by their Oppression. They have by their subtle imaginary and covetous wit, got the plain-hearted poor, or younger Brethren to work for them, for small wages, and by their work have got a great increase; for the poor by their labour lifts up Tyrants to rule over them; or else by their covetous wit, they have out-reached the plain-hearted in Buying and Selling, and thereby inriched themselves, but impoverished others: or else by their subtile wit, having been a lifter up into places of Trust, have inforced people to pay Money for a Publick use, but have divided much of it into their private purses; and so have got it by Oppression.

Then Secondly for Murther; They have by subtile wit and power, pretended to preserve a people in safety by the power of the Sword; and what by large Pay, much Free-quarter, and other Booties, which they call their own, they get much Monies, and with this they buy Land, and become landlords; and if once Landlords, then they rise to be Justices, Rulers, and State Governours, as experience shewes: But all this is but a bloudy and subtile Theevery, countenanced by a Law that Covetousness made; and is a breach of the Seventh Commandement, *Thou shalt not kill.*

And likewise Thirdly a breach of the Eighth Commandement, *Thou shalt not steal*; but these landlords have thus stoln the Earth from their fellow Creatures, that have an equal share with them, by the Law of Reason and Creation, as well as they.

And such as these rise up to be rich in the objects of the Earth; then by their plausible words of flattery to the plain-hearted people, whom they deceive, and that lies under confusion and blindness: They are lifted up to be Teachers, Rulers, and Law makers over them that lifted them up; as if the Earth were made peculiarly for them, and not for others weal: If you cast your eye a little backward, you shall see, That this outward Teaching and Ruling power, is the Babylonish yoke laid upon Israel of old, under *Nebuchadnezzar*; and so Successively from that time, the Conquering Enemy, have still laid these yokes upon Israel to keep *Iacob* down: And the last enslaving Conquest which the Enemy got over Israel, was the *Norman* over *England*; and from that time, Kings, Lords, Judges, Justices, Bayliffs, and the violent bitter people that are Free-holders, are and have been Successively. The *Norman* Bastard *William* himself, his Colonels, Captains, inferiour Officers, and Common souldiers, who still are from that time to this day in pursuite of that victory, Imprisoning, Robbing, and killing the poor enslaved *English* Israelites.[11]

And this appears cleer, For when any Trustee or State Officer is to be Chosen, The Free-holders or Landlords must be the Chusers, who are the *Norman* Common Souldiers, spread abroad in the Land; And who must be Chosen? but some very rich man, who is the Successor of the *Norman* Colonels or high Officers. And to what end have they been thus Chosen? but to Establish that *Norman* power the more forcibly over the enslaved *English*, and to beat them down again, when as they gather heart to seek for Liberty.

For what are all those Binding and Restraining Laws that have been made from one Age to another since that Conquest, and are still upheld by Furie over the People? I say, What are they? but the Cords, Bands, Manacles, and Yokes that the enslaved *English*, like *Newgate* Prisoners, wears upon their hands and legs as they walk the streets; by which those *Norman* Oppressors, and these their Successors from Age to Age have enslaved the poor People by, killed their younger Brother, and would not suffer *Iacob* to arise.

O what mighty Delusion, do you, who are the powers of *England* live in! That while you pretend to throw down that *Norman* yoke, and *Babylonish* power, and have promised to make the groaning people of *England* a Free People; yet you still lift up that *Norman* yoke, and slavish Tyranny, and holds the People as much in bondage, as the Bastard Conquerour himself, and his Councel of War.

Take notice, That *England* is not a Free People, till the Poor that have no Land, have a free allowance to dig and labour the Commons, and so live as Comfortably as the Landlords that live in their Inclosures. For the People have not laid out their Monies, and shed their Bloud, that their Landlords, the *Norman* power, should still have its liberty and freedom to rule in Tyranny in his Lords, landlords, Judges, Justices, Bayliffs, and State Servants; but that the Oppressed might be set Free, Prison doors opened, and the Poor peoples hearts comforted by an universal Consent of making the Earth a Common Treasury, that they may live together as one House of Israel, united in brotherly love into one Spirit; and having a comfortable livelihood in the Community of one Earth their Mother.

If you look through the Earth, you shall see, That the landlords, Teachers and Rulers, are Oppressors, Murtherers, and Theeves in this manner; But it was not thus from the Beginning. And this is one Reason of our digging and labouring the Earth one with another; That we might work in righteousness, and lift up the Creation from bondage: For so long as we own Landlords in this Corrupt Settlement, we cannot work in righteousness; for we should still lift up the Curse, and tread down the Creation, dishonour the Spirit of universal Liberty, and hinder the work of Restauration.

Secondly, In that we begin to Digge upon *George-Hill*, to eate our Bread together by righteous labour, and sweat of our browes, It was shewed us by Vision in Dreams, and out of Dreams, That that should be the Place we should begin upon; And though that Earth in view of Flesh, be very barren, yet we should trust the Spirit for a blessing. And that not only this Common, or Heath should be taken in and Manured by the People, but all the Commons and waste Ground in *England*, and in the whole World, shall be taken in by the People in righteousness, not owning any Propriety; but taking the Earth to be a Common Treasury, as it was first made for all.

Thirdly, It is shewed us, That all the Prophecies, Visions, and Revelations of Scriptures, of Prophets, and Apostles, concerning the calling of the Jews, the Restauration of Israel; and making of that People, the Inheritors of the whole Earth; doth all seat themselves in this Work of making the Earth a Common Treasury; as you may read, *Ezek.* 24.26, 27, &c. *Jer.* 33.7. to 12. *Esay.* 49.17, 18, &c. *Zach.* 8. from 4, to 12, *Dan.* 2.44,45. *Dan.* 7.27. *Hos.* 14.5,6,7. *Joel*2.26,27. *Amos* 9. from 8 to the end, *Obad.*17.18.21. *Mic.*5.from 7 to the end, *Hab.* 2.6,7,8, 13,14. *Gen.*18.18.*Rom.*11.15.*Zeph.*3.&c.*Zech.*14.9.

And when the Son of man, was gone from the Apostles, his Spirit descended upon the Apostles and Brethren, as they were waiting at *Ierusalem*; and the Rich men sold their Possessions, and gave part to the Poor; and no man said, That ought that he possesed was his own, for they had all things Common, *Act.*4.32.

Now this Community was supprest by covetous proud flesh, which was the powers that ruled the world; and the righteous Father suffered himself thus to be suppressed for a time, times and dividing of time, or for 42 months, or for three days and half, which are all but one and the same term of time: And the world is now come to the half day; and the Spirit of Christ, which is the Spirit of universal Community and Freedom is risen, and is rising, and will rise higher and higher, till those pure waters of *Shiloe*, the Well Springs of Life and Liberty to the whole Creation, do over-run *A-dam*, and drown those banks of Bondage, Curse, and Slavery.

Fourthly, This work to make the Earth a Common Treasury, was shewed us by Voice in Trance, and out of Trance, which words were these,

Work together, Eate Bread together, Declare this all abroad.

Which Voice was heard Three times: And in Obedience to the Spirit, We have Declared this by Word of mouth, as occasion was offered. Secondly, We have declared it by writing, which others may reade. Thirdly, We have now begun to declare it by Action, in Diging up the Common Land, and casting in Seed, that we may eat our Bread together in righteousness. And every one that comes to work, shall eate the Fruit of their own labours, one having as much Freedom in the Fruit of the Earth as another. Another Voice that was heard was this,

Israel shall neither take Hire, nor give Hire.

And if so, then certainly none shall say, This is my Land, work for me, and I'le give you Wages. For, The Earth is the Lords, that is, Mans, who is Lord of the Creation, in every branch of mankind; for as divers members of our human bodies, make but one body perfect; so every particular man is but a member or branch of mankind; and mankind living in the light and obedience to Reason, the King of righteousness, is thereby made a fit and compleat Lord of the Creation. And the whole Earth is this Lords Man, subject to the Spirit. And not the Inheritance of covetous proud Flesh, that is selvish, and enmity to the Spirit.

And if the Earth be not peculiar to any one branch, or branches of mankind, but the Inheritance of all; Then is it Free and Common for all, to work together, and eate together.

And truly, you Counsellors and Powers of the Earth, know this, That wheresoever there is a People, thus united by Common Community of livelihood into Oneness, it will become the strongest Land in the World, for then they will be as one man to defend their Inheritance; and Salvation (which is Liberty and Peace) is the Walls and Bulwarks of that Land or City.

Whereas on the otherside, pleading for Propriety and single Interest, divides the People of a land, and the whole world into Parties, and is the cause of all Wars and Bloud-shed, and Contention every where.

Another Voice that was heard in a Trance, was this,

Whosoever labours the Earth for any Person or Persons, that are lifted up to rule over others, and doth not look upon themselves, as Equal to others in the Creation: The hand of the Lord shall be upon that Laborer: I the Lord have spoke it, and I will do it.

This Declares likewise to all Laborers, or such as are called Poor people, that they shall not dare to work for Hire, for any Landlord, or for any that is lifted up above others; for by their labours, they have lifted up Tyrants and Tyranny; and by denying to labor for Hire, they shall pull them down again. He that works for another, either for Wages, or to pay him Rent, works unrighteously, and still lifts up the Curse; but they that are resolved to work and eat together, making the Earth a Common Treasury, doth joyn hands with Christ, to lift up the Creation from Bondage, and restores all things from the Curse.

Fiftly, That which does incourage us to go on in this work, is this; we find the streaming out of Love in our hearts towards all; to enemies as well as friends; we would have none live in

Beggery, Poverty, or Sorrow, but that everyone might enjoy the benefit of his creation: we have peace in our hearts, and quiet rejoycing in our work, and filled with sweet content, though we have but a dish of roots and bread for our food.

And we are assured, that in the strength of this Spirit that hath manifested himself to us, we shall not be startled, neither at Prison nor Death, while we are about his work; and we have bin made to sit down and count what it may cost us in undertaking such a work, and we know the full sum, and are resolved to give all that we have to buy this Pearl which we see in the Field.

For by this work we are assured, and Reason makes it appear to others, that Bondage shall be removed, Tears wiped away, and all poor People by their righteous Labours shall be relieved, and freed from Poverty and Straits; For in this work of Restoration there will be no begger in Israel: For surely, if there was no Begger in literal Israel, there shall be no Begger in Spiritual Israel the Anti-type, much more.

Sixtly, We have another encouragement that this work shall prosper, Because we see it to be the fulness of Time: For whereas the Son of Man, the *Lamb*, came in the Fulness of Time, that is, when the Powers of the World made the Earth stink every where, by oppressing others, under pretense of worshipping the Spirit rightly, by the Types and Sacrifices of *Moses* law; the Priests were grown so abominably Covetous and Proud, that they made the People to loathe the Sacrifices and to groan under the Burden of their Oppressing Pride.

Even so now in this Age of the World, that the Spirit is upon his Resurrection, it is likewise the Fulness of Time in a higher measure. For whereas the People generally in former times did rest upon the very observation of the Sacrifices and Types, but persecuted the very name of the Spirit; Even so now, Professors[12] do rest upon the bare observation of Forms and Customs, and pretend to the Spirit, and yet persecutes, grudges, and hates the power of the Spirit; and as it was then, so it is now: All places stink with the abomination of Self-seeking Teachers and Rulers. For do not I see that everyone Preacheth for money, Counsels for money, and fights for money to maintain particular Interests? And none of these three, that pretend to give liberty to the Creation, do give liberty to the Creation; neither can they, for they are enemies to universal liberty; So that the earth stinks with their Hypocrisie, Covetousness, Envie, sottish Ignorance, and Pride.

The common People are filled with good words from Pulpits and Councel Tables, but no good Deeds; For they wait and wait for good, and for deliverances, but none comes; While they wait for liberty, behold greater bondage comes instead of it, and burdens, oppressions, taskmasters, from Sessions, Lawyers, Bayliffs of Hundreds, Committees, Impropriators, Clerks of Peace, and Courts of Justice, so called, does whip the People by old Popish weather-beaten Laws, that were excommunicate long ago by Covenants, Oaths, and Ordinances; but as yet are not cast out, but rather taken in again, to be standing pricks in our eys, and thorns in our side; Beside Free-quartering, Plundering by some rude Souldiers, and the abounding of Taxes; which if they were equally divided among the Souldiery, and not too much bagd up in the hands of particular Officers and Trustees, there would be less complaining: Besides the horrible cheating that is in Buying and Selling, and the cruel Oppression of Landlords, and Lords of Mannours, and quarter Sessions; Many that have bin good House-keepers (as we say) cannot live, but are forced to turn Souldiers, and so to fight to uphold the Curse, or else live in great straits and beggery: O you *A-dams* of the Earth, you have rich Clothing, full Bellies, have your Honors and Ease, and you puffe at this; But know thou stout-hearted *Pharoah*, that the day of Judgement is begun, and it will reach to thee ere long; *Jacob* hath bin very low, but he is rising, and will rise, do the worst thou canst; and the poor people whom thou oppresses, shall be the Saviours of the land; For the blessing is rising up in them, and thou shalt be ashamed.

And thus, you Powers of England, and of the whole World, we have declared our Reasons, why we have begun to dig upon *George* hill in Surrey. One thing I must tell you more, in the close, which I received *in voce* likewise at another time; and when I received it, my ey was set towards you. The words were these:

Let Israel go free.

Surely, as Israel lay 430. years under *Pharoahs* bondage, before *Moses* was sent to fetch them out: even so Israel (the Elect Spirit spread in Sons and Daughters) hath lain three times so long already, which is the Anti-type, under your Bondage, and cruel Task-masters: But now the time of Deliverance is come, and thou proud *Esau*, and stout-hearted Covetousness, thou must come down, and be lord of the Creation no longer. For *now the King of Righteousness is rising to Rule In, and Over the Earth.*

Therefore, if thou wilt find Mercy, *Let Israel go Free*; break in pieces quickly the Band of particular Propriety, dis-own this oppressing Murder, Oppression and Thievery of Buying and Selling of Land, owning of landlords, and paying of Rents, and give thy Free Consent to make the Earth a Common Treasury, without grumbling; That the younger Brethren may live comfortably upon Earth, as well as the Elder: That all may enjoy the benefit of their Creation.

And hereby thou wilt *Honour thy Father, and thy Mother.* Thy Father, which is the Spirit of Community, that made all, and that dwels in all. Thy Mother, which is the Earth, that brought us all forth: That as a true Mother, loves all her Children. Therefore do not thou hinder the Mother Earth, from giving all her Children suck, by thy Inclosing it into particular hands, and holding up that cursed Bondage of Inclosure by thy Power.

And then thou wilt repent of thy *Theft*, in maintaining the breach of the eight Commandment, by *Stealing* the Land as I say from thy fellow-creatures, or younger Brothers: which thou and all thy landlords have, and do live in the breach of that Commandment.

Then thou wilt *Own no other God*, or Ruling Power, *but One*, which is the King of Righteousness, ruling and dwelling in every one, and in the whole; whereas now thou hast many gods: For Covetousness is thy God, Pride, and an Envious murdering Humor (to kill one by Prison or Gallows, that crosses thee, though their cause be pure, sound, and good reason) is thy God, Self-love, and slavish Fear (lest others serve thee as thou hast served them) is thy god, Hypocrisie, Fleshly Imagination, that keeps no Promise, Covenant, nor Protestation, is thy God: love of Money, Honor, and Ease, is thy God: And all these, and the like Ruling Powers, makes thee Blind, and hard-hearted, that thou does not, nor cannot lay to heart the affliction of others, though they dy for want of bread, in that rich City, undone under your eys.

Therefore once more, *Let Israel go Free*, that the poor may labour the Waste land, and suck the Brests of their mother *Earth*, that they starve not: And in so doing, thou wilt keep the *Sabbath day*, which is a day of *Rest*; sweetly enjoying the Peace of the Spirit of Righteousness; and find Peace, by living among a people that live in peace; this will be a day of *Rest* which thou never knew yet.

But I do not entreat thee, for thou art not to be intreated, but in the *Name of the Lord*, that hath drawn me forth to speak to thee; I, yea I say, I Command thee, to *let Israel go Free*, and quietly *to gather together into the place where I shall appoint; and hold them no longer in bondage.*

And thou *A-dam* that holds the Earth in slavery under the Curse: If thou wilt not *let Israel go Free*; for thou being the Antitype, will be more stout and lusty then the *Egyptian Pharoah* of old, who was thy Type; Then know, That whereas I brought *Ten* Plagues upon him, I will *Multiply* my Plagues upon thee, till

I make thee weary, and miserably ashamed: And *I will bring out my People with a strong hand, and stretched out arme.*

Thus we have discharged our Souls in declaring the Cause of our Digging upon *George-Hill* in *Surrey*, that the Great Councel and Army of the Land may take notice of it, That there is no intent of Tumult or Fighting, but only to get Bread to eat, with the sweat of our brows; working together in righteousness, and eating the blessings of the Earth in peace.

And if any of you that are the great Ones of the Earth, that have been bred tenderly, and cannot work, do bring in your Stock into this Common Treasury as an Offering to the work of Righteousness; we will work for you, and you shall receive as we receive. But if you will not, but *Pharoah* like, cry, *Who is the Lord that we should obey him?* and endeavour to Oppose, then know, That he that delivered Israel from *Pharoah* of old, is the same Power still, in whom we trust, and whom we serve; for this Conquest over thee shall be got, *not by Sword or Weapon, but by my Spirit saith the Lord of Hosts.*

	Ferrard Winstanley,
William Everard,	*Richard Goodgroome,*
Iohn Palmer,	*Thomas Starre,*
Iohn South,	*William Hoggrill,*
Iohn Courton,	*Robert Sawyer,*
William Taylor,	*Thomas Eder,*
Christopher Clifford,	*Henry Bickerstaffe,*
Iohn Barker.	*John Taylor,* &c.

FINIS.

NOTES

1. The Digger colony on St George's Hill commenced on 1 April 1649. The preface to this manifesto is dated 20 April, the day that Winstanley and William Everard appeared before Lord Fairfax in London. Everard was a former radical in the New Model Army, cashiered after the mutiny at Ware in 1647. He disappears from the Digger records after these early appearances.

2. Contentation: contented.

3. Thought to hail from a middling Walton family. Perhaps a recent convert, suggests Berens (p. 99): his name is last on the list. John Taylor had a namesake among the local opponents of the Diggers.

4. On enclosures see the Foreword.

5. Either a reference to a particular pledge—the Act abolishing the monarchy (17 March 1649) promises 'the lasting freedom and good of this Commonwealth', for example—or alternatively, an encapsulation of the many declarations advanced in the parliamentary cause.

6. The Solemn League and Covenant taken by the Commons on 25 September 1643 sealed an Anglo-Scottish military alliance against the royalists. It pledged 'a real reformation' across the Stuart kingdoms. Parliament required all Englishmen to subscribe it. Winstanley took the Covenant on 8 October, but with the Diggers he risks official wrath by interpreting 'a real reformation' in his own manner.

7. Winstanley may have in mind the removal of the hated prerogative courts of Star Chamber and High Commission in 1641.

8. Sizes: Assizes.

9. Compulsory provision of free board and lodging for soldiers, much called upon in Cobham by troops passing to and from London.

10. The New Model Army, created in 1645, was the great hope of Civil War radicals: 'not a mere mercenary army' but one committed 'to the defence of our own and the people's just rights and liberties', said *A Declaration from Sir Thomas Fairfax and the Army* in 1647. The Council of State, executive arm of the new Commonwealth, dates from 13 February 1649.

11. On the Norman Yoke see the Foreword.

12. Professors: those who profess to be religious.

A

DECLARATION

FROM THE

Poor oppressed People

OF

ENGLAND,

DIRECTED
To all that call themselves, or are called

Lords of Manors,

through this NATION;
That have begun to cut, or that through
fear and covetousness, do intend to cut down
the Woods and Trees that grow upon the
Commons and Waste Land.[1]

Printed in the Yeer, 1649.

A DECLARATION FROM THE POOR
OPPRESSED PEOPLE OF *ENGLAND*

We whose names are subscribed, do in the name of all the poor oppressed people in England, declare unto you, that call your selves Lords of Manors, and Lords of the Land, That in regard the King of Righteousness, our Maker, hath inlightened our hearts so far, as to see, That the earth was not made purposely for you, to be Lords of it, and we to be your Slaves, Servants, and Beggers; but it was made to be a common Livelihood to all, without respect of persons: And that your buying and selling of Land, and the Fruits of it, one to another, is The cursed thing, and was brought in by War; which hath, and still does establish murder, and theft, in the hands of some branches of Mankinde over others, which is the greatest outward burden, and unright-eous power, that the Creation groans under: For the power of inclosing Land, and owning Propriety, was brought into the Creation by your Ancestors by the Sword; which first did mur-ther their fellow Creatures, Men, and after plunder or steal away their Land, and left this Land successively to you, their Children. And therefore, though you did not kill or theeve, yet you hold that cursed thing in your hand, by the power of the Sword; and so you justifie the wicked deeds of your Fathers; and that sin of your Fathers, shall be visited upon the Head of you, and your Children, to the third and fourth Generation, and longer too, till your bloody and theeving power be rooted out of the Land.

And further, in regard the King of Righteousness hath made us sensible of our burthens, and the cryes and groanings of our hearts are come before him: We take it as a testimony of love from him, That our hearts begin to be freed from slavish fear of men, such as you are; and that we find Resolutions in us, grounded upon the inward law of Love, one towards another, To Dig and Plough up the Commons, and waste Lands through *England*; and that our conversation shall be so unblameable, That your Laws shall not reach to oppress us any longer, unless you by your Laws will shed the innocent blood that runs in our veins.

For though you and your Ancestors got your Propriety by murther and theft, and you keep it by the same power from us, that have an equal right to the Land with you, by the righteous Law of Creation, yet we shall have no occasion of quarrelling (as you do) about that disturbing devil, called *Particular Propriety*: For the Earth, with all her Fruits of Corn, Cattle, and such like, was made to be a common Store-house of Livelihood to all Mankinde, friend, and foe, without exception.

And to prevent your scrupulous Objections, know this, That we must neither buy nor sell; Money must not any longer (after our work of the Earths community is advanced) be the great god, that hedges in some, and hedges out others; for Money is but part of the Earth: And surely, the Righteous Creator, who is King, did never ordain, That unless some of Mankinde, do bring that Mineral (Silver and Gold) in their hands, to others of their own kinde, that they should neither be fed, nor be clothed; no surely, For this was the project of Tyrant-flesh (which Land-lords are branches of) to set his Image upon Money. And they make this unrighteous Law, That none should buy or sell, eat, or be clothed, or have any comfortable Livelihood among men, unless they did bring his Image stamped upon Gold or Silver in their hands.

And whereas the Scriptures speak, That the mark of the Beast is 666, the number of a man; and that those that do not bring that mark in their hands, or in their foreheads, they should neither buy not sell, *Revel.* 13.16. And seeing the numbering Letters round about the English money make 666,[2] which is the number of that Kingly Power and Glory, (called a *Man*) And seeing the age of the Creation is now come to the Image of the Beast, or Half day. And seeing 666 is his mark, we expect this to be the last Tyrannical power that shall raign; and that people shall live freely in the enjoyment of the Earth, without bringing the mark of the Beast in their hands, or in their promise; and that they shall buy Wine and Milk, without Money, or without price, as *Isiah* speaks.

For after our work of the Earthly community is advanced, we must make use of Gold and Silver, as we do of other metals, but not to buy and sell withal; for buying and selling is the great cheat, that robs and steals the Earth one from another: It is that which makes some Lords, others Beggers, some Rulers, others to be ruled; and makes great Murderers and Theeves to be imprisoners, and hangers of little ones, or of sincere-hearted men.

And while we are made to labor the Earth together, with one consent and willing minde; and while we are made free, that every one, friend and foe, shall enjoy the benefit of their Creation, that is, To have food and rayment from the Earth, their Mother; and every one subject to give accompt of his thoughts, words, and actions to none, but to the one onely righteous Judg, and Prince of Peace; the Spirit of Righteousness that dwells, and that is now rising up to rule in every Creature, and in the whole Globe. We say, while we are made to hinder no man of his Priviledges given him in his Creation, equal to one, as to another; what Law then can you make, to take hold upon us, but Laws of Oppression and Tyranny, that shall enslave or spill the blood of the Innocent? And so your Selves, your

Judges, Lawyers, and Justices, shall be found to be the greatest
Transgressors, in, and over Mankinde.

But to draw neerer to declare our meaning, what we would have,
and what we shall endevor to the uttermost to obtain, as moderate
and righteous Reason directs us; seeing we are made to see our
Priviledges, given us in our Creation, which have hitherto been
denied to us, and our Fathers, since the power of the Sword began
to rule, And the secrets of the Creation have been locked up under
the traditional, Parrat-like speaking, from the Universities, and
Colledges for Scholars, And since the power of the murdering, and
theeving Sword, formerly, as well as now of late yeers, hath set up a
Government, and maintains that Government; for what are prisons,
and putting others to death, but the power of the Sword to enforce
people to that Government which was got by Conquest and Sword,
and cannot stand of it self, but by the same murdering power? That
Government that is got over people by the Sword and kept by the
Sword, is not set up by the King of Righteousness to be his Law,
but by Covetousness, the great god of the world; who hath been
permitted to raign for a time, times, and dividing of time, and his
government draws to the period of the last term of his allotted time;
and then the Nations shall see the glory of that Government that
shall rule in Righteousness, without either Sword or Spear,

And seeing further, the power of Righteousness in our hearts,
seeking the Livelihood of others as well as our selves, hath drawn
forth our bodies to begin to dig, and plough, in the Commons
and waste Land, for the Reasons already declared,

And seeing and finding ourselves poor, wanting Food to feed
upon, while we labor the Earth to cast in Seed, and to wait till
the first Crop comes up; and wanting Ploughs, Carts, Corn, and
such materials to plant the Commons withal, we are willing to
declare our condition to you, and to all, that have the Treasury
of the Earth, locked up in your Bags, Chests, and Barns, and will
offer up nothing to this publike Treasury; but will rather see your
fellow Creatures starve for want of Bread, that have an equal right

to it with your selves, by the Law of Creation: But this by the way we onely declare to you, and to all that follow the subtle art of buying and selling the Earth, with her Fruits, meerly to get the Treasury thereof into their hands, to lock it up from them, to whom it belongs; that so, such covetous, proud, unrighteous, selfish flesh, may be left without excuse in the day of Judgment.

And therefore, the main thing we aym at, and for which we declare our Resolutions to go forth, and act, is this, To lay hold upon, and as we stand in need, to cut and fell, and make the best advantage we can of the Woods and Trees, that grow upon the Commons, To be a stock for our selves, and our poor Brethren, through the land of *England*, to plant the Commons withal; and to provide us bread to eat, till the Fruit of our labors in the Earth bring forth increase; and we shall meddle with none of your Proprieties (but what is called Commonage) till the Spirit in you, make you cast up your Lands and Goods, which were got, and still is kept in your hands by murder, and theft; and then we shall take it from the Spirit, that hath conquered you, and not from our Swords, which is an abominable, and unrighteous power, and a destroyer of the Creation: But the Son of man comes not to destroy, but to save.

And we are moved to send forth this Declaration abroad, to give notice to every one whom it concerns, in regard we hear and see, that some of you, that have been Lords of Manors, do cause the Trees and Woods that grow upon the Commons, which you pretend a Royalty unto, to be cut down and sold, for your own private use, whereby the Common Land, which your own mouths doe say belongs to the poor, is impoverished, and the poor oppressed people robbed of their Rights, while you give them cheating words, by telling some of our poor oppressed Brethren, That those of us that have begun to Dig and Plough up the Commons, will hinder the poor; and so blinde their eyes, that they see not their Priviledge, while you, and the rich Free-holders make the most profit of the Commons, by your over-stocking of them with Sheep and Cattle; and the poor that have the name to own the Commons, have the least share therein; nay, they are checked by you, if they cut Wood, Heath, Turf, or Furseys, in places about the Common, where you disallow.

Therefore we are resolved to be cheated no longer, nor be held under the slavish fear of you no longer, seing the Earth was made for us, as well as for you: And if the Common Land belongs to us who are the poor oppressed, surely the woods that grow upon the Commons belong to us likewise: therefore we are resolved to try the uttermost in the light of reason, to know whether we shall be free men, or slaves. If we lie still, and let you steale away our birthrights, we perish; and if we Petition we perish also, though we have paid taxes, given free quarter, and ventured our lives to preserve the Nations freedom as much as you, and therefore by the law of contract with you, freedom in the land is our portion as well as yours, equal with you: And if we strive for freedom, and your murdering, governing Laws destroy us, we can but perish.

Therefore we require, and we resolve to take both Common Land, and Common woods to be a livelihood for us, and look upon you as equal with us, not above us, knowing very well, that *England* the land of our Nativity, is to be a common Treasury of livelihood to all, without respect of persons.

So then, we declare unto you, that do intend to cut our Common Woods and Trees, that you shall not do it; unlesse it be for a stock for us, as aforesaid, and we to know of it, by a publick declaration abroad, that the poor oppressed, that live thereabouts, may take it, and employ it, for their publike use, therefore take notice we have demanded it in the name of the Commons of *England*, and of all the Nations of the world, it being the righteous freedom of the Creation.

Likewise we declare to you that have begun to cut down our Common Woods and Trees, and to fell and carry away the same for your private use, that you shall forbear, and go no farther, hoping, that none that are friends to the Commonwealth of England, will endeavour to buy any of those Common Trees and Woods of any of those Lords of Mannors, so called, who have, by the murdering and cheating law of the sword, stolen the Land from younger brothers, who have by the law of Creation, a standing portion in the Land, as well, and equall with others. Therefore we hope all Wood-mongers will disown all such private merchandize, as being a robbing of the poor oppressed, and take notice, that they have been told our resolution: But if any of you that are Wood-mongers, will buy it of the poor, and for their use, to stock the Commons, from such as may be appointed by us to sell it, you shall have it quietly, without diminution; but if you will slight us in this thing, blame us not, if we make stop of the Carts you send and convert the Woods to our own use, as need requires, it being our own, equal with him that calls himself the Lord of the Mannor, and not his peculiar right, shutting us out, but he shall share with us as a fellow-creature.

For we say our purpose is, to take those Common Woods to sell them, now at first, to be a stock for our selves, and our children after us, to plant and manure the Common land withall; for we shall endeavour by our righteous acting not to leave the earth any longer intangled unto our children, by self-seeking proprietors; But to leave it a free store-house, and common treasury to all, without respect of persons; And this we count is our dutie, to endeavour to the uttermost, every man in his place (according to the nationall Covenant which the Parliament set forth) a Reformation to preserve the peoples liberties, one as well as another: As well those as have paid taxes, and given free quarter, as those that have either born the sword, or taken our moneys to dispose of them for publike use: for if the Reformation must be according to the word of God,[3] then every one is to have the benefit and freedom of his creation, without respect of persons; we count this our duty, we say, to endeavour to the uttermost, and so shall leave those that rise up to oppose us without excuse, in their day of Judgment; and our precious blood, we hope, shall not be dear to us, to be willingly laid down at the door of a prison, or foot of a gallows, to justifie this righteous cause; if those that have taken our money from us, and promised to give us freedom for it, should turn Tyrants against us: for we must not fight, but suffer.

And further we intend, that not one, two, or a few men of us shall sell or exchange the said woods, but it shall be known publikly in Print or writing to all, how much every such, and such parcell of wood is sold for, and how it is laid out, either in victualls, corn, ploughs, or other materials necessary.

And we hope we may not doubt (at least we expect) that they that are called the great Councel and powers of *England*, who so often have declared themselves, by promises and Convenants, and confirmed them by multitude of fasting daies, and devout Protestations, to make *England* a free people, upon condition they would pay moneys, and adventure their lives against the successor of the *Norman* Conqueror; under whose oppressing power *England* was enslaved; And we look upon that freedom promised to be the inheritance of all, without respect of persons; And this cannot be, unless the Land of *England* be freely set at liberty from proprietors, and become a common Treasury to all her children, as every portion of the Land of *Canaan* was the Common livelihood of such and such a Tribe, and of every member in that Tribe, without exception, neither hedging in any, nor hedging out.

We say we hope we need not doubt of their sincerity to us herein, and that they will not gainsay our determinate course; howsoever, their actions will prove to the view of all, either their sinceritie, or hypocrisie: We know what we speak is our priviledge, and our cause is righteous, and if they doubt of it, let them but send a childe for us to come before them, and we shall make it manifest four wayes.

First, by the National Covenant, which yet stands in force to bind Parliament and people to be faithful and sincere, before the Lord God Almighty, wherein every one in his several place hath covenanted to preserve and seek the liberty each of other, without respect of persons.

Secondly, by the late Victory over King *Charls*, we do claime this our priviledge, to be quietly given us, out of the hands of Tyrant-Government, as our bargain and contract with them; for the Parliament promised, if we would pay taxes, and give free quarter, and adventure our lives against *Charls* and his party, whom they called the Common enemy, they would make us a free people; These three being all done by us, as well as by themselves, we claim this our bargain, by the law of contract from them, to be a free people with them, and to have an equall priviledge of Common livelihood with them, they being chosen by us, but for a peculiar worke, and for an appointed time, from among us, not to be our oppressing Lords, but servants to succour us. But these two are our weakest proofs. And yet by them (in the light of reason and equity that dwells in mens hearts) we shall with ease cast down, all those former enslaving *Norman* reiterated laws, in every Kings raigne since the Conquest, which are as thornes in our eyes, and pricks in our sides, and which are called the Ancient Government of *England*.

Thirdly, we shall prove, that we have a free right to the land of *England*, being born, therein as well as elder brothers, and that it is our right equal with them, and they with us, to have a comfortable livelihood in the earth, without owning any of our own kinde, to be either Lords, or Land-Lords over us: And this we shall prove by plain Text of Scripture, without exposition upon them, which the Scholars and great ones generally say, is their rule to walk by.

Fourthly, we shall prove it by the Righteous Law of our Creation, That mankinde in all his branches, is the Lord of the Earth and ought not to be in subjection to any of his own kinde without him, but to live in the light of the law of righteousness, and peace established in his heart.

And thus in love we have declared the purpose of our hearts plainly, without flatterie, expecting love, and the same sincerity from you, without grumbling or quarreling, being Creatures of your own Image and mould, intending no other matter herein, but to observe the Law of righteous action, endeavouring to shut out of the Creation, the cursed thing, called *Particular Propriety*, which is the cause of all wars, bloud-shed, theft, and enslaving Laws, that hold the people under miserie.

Signed for and in behalf of all the poor oppressed people of *England*, and the whole world.

Gerrard Winstanley	*James Manley*	*Iohn Ash*
Iohn Coulton	*Thomas Barnard*	*Ralph Ayer*
Iohn Palmer	*Iohn South*	*Iohn Pra*
Thomas Star	*Robert Sayer*	*Iohn Wilkinson*
Samuel Webb	*Christopher Clifford*	*Anthony Spire*
Iohn Hayman	*Iohn Beechee*	*Thomas East*
Thomas Edcer	*William Coomes*	*Allen Brown*
William Hogrill	*Christopher Boncher*	*Edward Parret*
Daniel Weeden	*Richard Taylor*	*Richard Gray*
Richard Wheeler	*Urian Worthington*	*Iohn Mordy*
Nathaniel Yates	*Nathaniel Holcombe*	*Iohn Bachilor*
William Clifford	*Giles Childe,* senior	*William Childe*
Iohn Harrison	*Iohn Webb*	*William Hatham*
Thomas Hayden	*Thomas Yarwel*	*Edward Wicher*
James Hall	*William Bonnington*	*William Tench.*

FINIS.

NOTES

1. The second Digger manifesto, published on or before 1 June 1649.
2. George H. Sabine suggests that Winstanley manoeuvred the abbreviated Latin inscription on Caroline coins to obtain the letters MDCLXVI, then ignored the M to create 666, *The Works of Gerrard Winstanley*, p. 270n.
3. Winstanley is making mischief with the Anglo-Scottish Solemn League and Covenant (1643), which pledged a reformation in England 'according to the word of God, and the example of the best reformed churches'—a ruse of the English parliamentarians to avoid outright commitment to Scottish Presbyterianism. See also p. 25, n6.

A
LETTER

TO

The Lord Fairfax,

AND

His Councell of War,

WITH
Divers Questions to the Lawyers, and Ministers:
Proving it an undeniable Equity,
That the common People ought to dig,
plow, plant and dwell upon the Commons, without hiring them, or paying Rent to any.[1]
Delivered to the Generall and the chief Officers on Saturday June 9.

By *Jerrard Winstanly*, in the behalf of those who have begun to dig upon *George*-Hill in Surrey.

London: Printed for *Giles Calvert*, at the black Spread-Eagle at the West end of P A U L S.   1 6 4 9 .

TO THE LORD FAIRFAX, GENERALL OF THE ENGLISH FORCES, AND HIS COUNCELL OF WAR.

SIR,
Our digging and ploughing upon *George*-hill in Surrey is not unknown to you, since you have seen some of our persons, and heard us speak in defence thereof: and we did receive mildnesse and moderation from you and your Councell of Warre, both when some of us were at White-hall before you, and when you came in person to *George*-hill to view our works; we indeavour to lay open the bottome and intent of our businesse, as much as can be, that none may be troubled with doubtfull imaginations about us, but may be satisfied in the sincerity and universall righteousnesse of the work.

We understand, that our digging upon that Common, is the talk of the whole Land; some approving, some disowning, some are friends, filled with love, and sees the worke intends good to the Nation, the peace whereof is that which we seeke after; others are enemies filled with fury, and falsely report of us, that we have intent to fortifie our selves, and afterwards to fight against others, and take away their goods from them, which is a thing we abhor: and many other slanders we rejoyce over, because we know ourselves cleare, our endeavour being no otherwise, but to improve the Commons, and to cast off that oppression and outward bondage which the Creation groans under, as much as in us lies, and to lift up and preserve the purity thereof.

And the truth is, experience shews us, that in this work of Community in the earth, and in the fruits of the earth, is seen plainly a pitched battaile between the Lamb and the Dragon, between the Spirit of love, humility and righteousnesse, which is the Lamb appearing in flesh; and the power of envy, pride, and unrighteousnesse, which is the Dragon appearing in flesh, the latter power striving to hold the Creation under slavery, and to lock and hide the glory thereof from man: the former power labouring to deliver the Creation from slavery, to unfold the secrets of it to the Sons of Men, and so to manifest himselfe to be the great restorer of all things.

And these two powers strive in the heart of every single man, & make single men to strive in opposition one against the other, and these strivings will be till the Dragon be cast out, and his judgement and downfall hastens apace, therefore let the right-eous hearts wait with patience upon the Lord, to see what end he makes of all the confused hurley burleys of the world.

When you were at our Works upon the Hill, we told you, many of the Countrey-people that were offended at first, begin now to be moderate, and to see righteousnesse in our work, and to own it, excepting one or two covetous Free-holders, that would have all the Commons to themselves, and that would uphold the Norman Tyranny over us, which by the victorie that you have got over the Norman Successor, is plucked up by the roots, therefore ought to be cast away. And we expect, that these our angry neighbours, whom we never wronged, nor will not wrong, will in time see their furious rashnesse to be their folly, and become moderate, to speak and carry themselves like men rationally, and leave off pushing with their hornes like beasts: they shall have no cause to say wee wrong them, unlesse they count us wrongers of them for seeking a livelihood out of the common Land of England by our righteous labour, which is our freedome, as we are Englishmen equall with them, and rather our freedome then theirs, because they are elder brothers and Free-holders, and call the Inclosures their own land, and we are younger brothers, and the poore oppressed, and the Common Lands are called ours, by their owne confession.

We told you (upon a question you put to us) that we were not against any that would have Magistrates and Laws to govern, as the Nations of the world are governed, but as for our parts we shall need neither the one nor the other in that nature of Government; for as our Land is common, so our Cattell is to be common, and our corn and fruits of the earth common, and are not to be brought and sold among us, but to remaine a standing portion of livelihood to us and our children, without that cheating intanglement of buying and selling, and we shall not arrest one another.

And then, what need have we of imprisoning, whipping, or hanging Laws, to bring one another into bondage? and we know that none of those that are subject to this righteous law dares arrest or inslave his brother for, or about the objects of the earth, because the earth is made by our Creator to be a common Treasury of livelihood to one equall with another, *without resect of persons.*

But now if you that are elder brothers, and that call the Inclosures your own land, hedging out others, if you will have Magistrates and Laws in this outward manner of the Nations, we are not against it, but freely without disturbance shall let you alone; and if any of we Commoners, or younger Brothers, shall steal your corne, or cattell, or pull down your hedges, let your laws take hold upon any of us that so offends.

But while we keep within the bounds of our Commons, and none of us shall be found guilty of medling with your goods, or inclosed proprieties, unlesse the Spirit in you freely give it up, your laws then shall not reach to us, unlesse you will oppresse or shed the blood of the innocent: and yet our corn and cattell shall not be locked up, as though we would be propriators in the middle of the Nation: no, no, we freely declare, that our corn and cattell, or what we have, shall be freely laid open, for the safety and preservation of the Nation, and we as younger brothers, living in love with you our elder brothers, for we shall endeavour to do, as we would be done unto; that is, to let every one injoy the benefit of his Creation, to have food and rayment free by the labour of his hands from the earth.

And as for spirituall teachings, we leave every man to stand and fall to his own Master: if the power of covetousnesse be his Master or King that rules in his heart, let him stand and fall to him; if the power of love and righteousnesse be his Master or King that rules in his heart, let him stand and fall to him; let the bodies of men act love, humility, and righteousnesse one towards another, and let the Spirit of righteousnesse be the Teacher, Ruler and Judge both in us and over us; and by thus doing, we shall honor our Father, the Spirit that gave us our being. And we shall honor our Mother the earth, by labouring her in righteous-nesse, and leaving her free from oppression and bondage.

We shall then honour the higher powers of the left hand man, which is our hearing, seeing, tasting, smelling, feeling, and walk in the light of reason and righteousnesse, that is, the King and Judge that sits upon this five cornered Throne, and we shall be strengthened by those five well springs of life, of the right hand man, which is, understanding, will, affections, joy and peace, and so live like men, in the light and power of the Son of righteousnesse within our selves feelingly. What need then have we of any outward, selfish, confused Laws made, to uphold the power of covetousnesse, when as we have the right-eous Law written in our hearts, teaching us to walk purely in the Creation.

Sir, The intent of our writing to you, is not to request your protection, though we have received an unchristian-like abuse from some of your souldiers; for truly we dare not cast off the Lord, and make choice of a man or men to rule us. For the Creation hath smarted deeply for such a thing, since Israel chose *Saul* to be their King; therefore we acknowledge before you in plain English, That we have chosen the Lord God Almighty to be our King and Protector.

Yet in regard you are our brethren (as an English Tribe) and for the present are owned to be the outward Governors, Protectors and Saviours of this Land, and whose hearts we question not, but that you endeavour to advance the same King of righteousnesse with us, therefore we are free to write to you, and to open the sincerity of our hearts freely to you, and to all the world.

And if after this report of ours, either you, or your Forces called souldiers, or any that owns your Laws of propriety, called freeholders, do abuse or kill our persons, we declare to you that we die, doing our duty to our Creator, by endeavouring from that power he hath put into our hearts to lift up his Creation out of bondage, and you and they shall be left without excuse in the day of Judgement, because you have been spoken to sufficiently.

And therefore our reason of writing to you is this, in regard some of your foot souldiers of the Generalls Regiment, under Captain *Stravie* that were quartered in our Town, we bearing part therein as well as our neighbours, giving them sufficient quarter, so that there was no complaining, did notwithstanding, go up to George-hill, where was onely one man and one boy of our company of the diggers. And at their first coming, divers of your souldiers, before any word of provocation was spoken to them, fell upon those two, beating the boy, and took away his coat off his back, and some linnen and victualls that they had, beating and wounding the man very dangerously, and fired our house.

Which we count a strange and Heathenish practise, that the souldierie should meddle with naked men, peaceable men, Countrymen, that meddled not with the souldiers businesse, nor offered any wrong to them in word or deed, unlesse, because we improve that victory which you have gotten in the name of the Commons over King *Charles*, do offend the souldierie. In doing whereof, we rather expect protection from you then destruction. But for your own particular, we are assured of your moderation and friendship to us, who have ever been your friends in times of straits; and that you would not give Commission to strike us, or fire and pull down our houses, but you would prove us an enemy first.

Yet we do not write this, that you should lay any punishment upon them, for that we leave to your discretion, only we desire (in the request of brethren) that you would send forth admonition to your souldiers, not to abuse us hereafter; unlesse they have a Commission from you; and truly if our offences should prove so great, you shall not need to send souldiers for us, or to beat us, for we shall freely come to you upon a bare letter.

Therefore that the ignorant, covetous, free-holders, and such of your ignorant souldiers, that know not what freedom is, may not abuse those that are true friends to Englands freedom, and faithfull servants to the Creation, we desire, that our businesse may be taken notice of by you, and the highest Councell the Parliament, and if our work appear righteous to you, as it does to us, and wherein our souls have sweet peace, in the midst of scandalls and abuses;

Then in the request of brethren, we desire we may injoy our freedom, according to the Law of contract between you and us, That we that are younger brothers, may live comfortably in the Land of our Nativity, with you the elder brothers, enjoying the benefit of our Creation, which is food and rayment freely by our labours; and that we may receive love, and the protection of brethren from you, seeing we have adventured estate and persons with you, to settle the Land in peace, and that we may not be abused by your Laws, nor by your souldiers, unlesse we break over into your inclosures as aforesaid, and take away your proprieties, before you are willing to deliver it up. And if this you do, we shall live in quietnesse, and the Nation will be brought into peace, while you that are the souldierie, are a wall of fire round about the Nation to keep a forraign enemy, and are succourers of your brethren that live within the Land, who indeavour to hold forth the Sun of righteousnesse in their actions, to the glory of our Creator.

And you and the Parliament hereby, will be faithfull in your Covenants, Oaths and promises to us, as we have been faithfull to you and them, in paying taxes, giving free-quarter, and affording other assistance in the publike work, whereby we that are the Common People, are brought almost to a morsell of bread, therefore we demand our bargain, which is freedome, with you in this Land of our Nativity.

But if you do sleight us and our cause, then know we shall not strive with sword and speare, but with spade and plow and such like instruments to make the barren and common Lands fruitful, and we have, and still shall, commit our selves and our cause unto our righteous King, whom we obey, even the Prince of peace to be our Protector; and unto whom you likewise professe much love, by your preaching, praying, fastings, and in whose name you have made all your Covenants, Oaths, and promises to us: I say unto him we appeal, who is and will be our righteous Judge, who never yet failed those that waited upon him, but ever did judge the cause of the oppressed righteously.

We desire that your Lawyers may consider these questions (which we affirm to be truths) and which gives good assurance by the Law of the Land, that we that are the younger brothers or common people, have a true right to dig, plow up and dwell upon the Commons, as we have declared.

1. Whether *William the Conqueror* became not to be King of England by conquest, turned the English out of their birthrights, burned divers townes, whereof thirty towns were burned by him in Windsore Forrest; by reason whereof all sorts of people suffered, and compelled the conquered English for necessity of livelihood to be servants to him and his Norman souldiers?

2. Whether King *Charles* was not successor to the Crown of England from *William the Conqueror*, and whether all Laws that have been made in every Kings Reign, did not confirm and strengthen the power of the Norman Conquest, and so did, and does still hold the Commons of England under slavery to the Kingly power, his Gentry and Clergie?

3. Whether Lords of Mannours were not the successors of the Colonells and chief Officers of *William the Conqueror*, and held their Royalty to the Commons by Lease, Grant and Patentee from the King, and the power of the sword was and is the seale to their Title?

4. Whether Lords of Mannours have not lost their Royalty to the common land, since the common People of England, as well as some of the Gentry, have conquered King *Charles*, and recovered themselves from under the Norman Conquest?

5. Whether the Norman Conqueror took the land of England to himself, out of the hands of a few men, called a Parliament, or from the whole body of the English People? Surely he took freedom from every one, and became the disposer both of inclosures and commons; therefore every one, upon the recovery of the conquest, ought to return into freedom again without respecting persons, or els what benefit shall the common people have (that have suffered most in these wars) by the victory that is got over the King? It had been better for the common people there had been no such conquest; for they are impoverished in their estates by Free-quarter and Taxes, and made worse to live then they were before. But seeing they have paid Taxes, and given Free-quarter according to their estates, as much as the

Gentry to theirs, it is both reason and equity that they should have the freedom of the land for their livelihood, which is the benefit of the commons, as the Gentry hath the benefit of their inclosures.

6. Whether the freedom which the common people have got, by casting out the Kingly power, lie not herein principally, to have the land of their nativity for their livelihood, freed from intanglement of Lords, Lords of Mannours, and Landlords, which are our task-masters. As when the enemy conquered England, he took the land for his own, and called that his freedom; even so, seeing all sorts of people have given assistance to recover England from under the Norman yoke, surely all sorts, both Gentry in their inclosures, Commonalty in their Commons, ought to have their freedom, not compelling one to work for wages for another.

7. Whether any Lawes since the coming in of Kings, have been made in the light of the righteous law of our creation, respecting all alike, or have not been grounded upon selfish principles, in feare or flattery of their King, to uphold freedom in the Gentry and Clergie, and to hold the common people under bondage still, and so respecting persons?

8. Whether all Lawes that are not grounded upon equity and reason, not giving a universal freedom to all, but respecting persons, ought not to be cut off with the Kings head? we affirm they ought.

If all lawes be grounded upon equity and reason, then the whole land of England is to be a common treasury to every one that is born in the land: But if they be grounded upon selfish principles, giving freedom to some, laying burdens upon others, such lawes are to be cut off with the Kings head; or els the neglecters are Covenant, Oaths and Promise-breakers, and open hypocrites to the whole world.

9. Whether every one without exception, by the law of contract, ought not to have liberty to enjoy the earth for his

livelihood, and to settle his dwelling in any part of the Commons of England, without buying or renting Land of any; seeing every one by Agreement and Covenant among themselves, have paid taxes, given free-quarter, and adventured their lives to recover England out of bondage? we affirm, they ought.

10. Whether the Laws that were made in the daies of the Kings, does give freedom to any other people, but to the gentry and Clergy, all the rest are left servants and bondmen to those task-masters; none have freedom by the Laws, but those two sorts of people, all the common people have been, and still are burdened under them.

And surely if the common people have no more freedom in England, but only to live among their elder brothers, and work for them for hire; what freedom then have they in England, more then we can have in Turkie of France? For there, if any man will work for wages, he may live among them, otherwise no: therefore consider, whether this be righteous, and for the peace of the Nation, that Laws shall be made to give freedom to impropriators and Free-holders, when as the poor that have no land, are left still in the straights of beggery, and are shut out of all livelihood, but what they shall pick out of sore bondage, by working for others, as Masters over them, and if this be not the burthen of the Norman yoke, let rationall men judge: therefore take not away men, but take away the power of tyranny and bad government, the price is in your hand, and let no part of the Nation be wronged for want of a Representative.

And here now we desire your publike Preachers, that say they preach the righteous law, to consider these questions, which confirms us in the peace of our hearts, that we that are the common people born in England, ought to improve the Commons, as we have declared, for a publike Treasury and live-lihood, and that those that hinder us are rebells to their Maker, and enemies to the Creation.

First, we demand I or No, whether the earth with her fruits, was made to be bought and sold from one to another? and whether one part of mankind was made a Lord of the land, and another part a servant, by the law of Creation before the fall?

I affirme, (and I challenge you to disprove) that the earth was made to be a common Treasury of livelihood for all, *without respect of persons*, and was not made to be bought and sold: And that mankind in all his branches, is the lord over the Beasts, Birds, Fishes, and the Earth, and was not made to acknowledge any of his owne kind to be his teacher and ruler, but the spirit of righteousnesse only his Maker, and to walk in his light, and so to live in peace, and this being a truth, as it is, then none ought to be Lords or Landlords over another, but the earth is free for every son and daughter of mankind, to live free upon.

This question is not to be answered by any text of Scripture, or example since the fall, but the answer is to be given in the light of it self, which is the law of righteousnesse, or that Word of God that was in the beginning, which dwells in mans heart, and by which he was made, even the pure law of creation, unto which the creation is to be restored.

Before the fall, *Adam*, or the Man did dresse the garden, or the earth, in love, freedom, and righteousnesse, which was his rest and peace: But when covetousnesse began to rise up in him, to kill the power of love and freedom in him, and so made him (mankind) to set himself one man above another, as *Cain* lifted up himself above *Abel*, which was but the outward declaration of the two powers that strive in the man *Adams* heart; and when he consented to that serpent covetousnesse, then he fell from righteousnesse, was cursed, and was sent into the earth to eat his bread in sorrow: And from that time began particular propriety to grow in one man over another; and the sword brought in pro-priety, and holds it up, which is no other but the power of angry covetousnesse: For, *Cain* killed *Abel*, because *Abels* principles, or religion, was contrary to his. And the power of the sword is still

Cain killing *Abel*, lifting up one man still above another. But *Abel* shall not alwaies be slain, nor alwaies lie under the bondage of *Cains* cursed propriety, for he must rise: And that *Abel* of old was but a type of *Christ*, that is now rising up to restore all things from bondage.

2. I demand, whether all wars, blood-shed, and misery came not upon the Creation, when one man indeavoured to be a lord over another, and to claime propriety in the earth one above another? your Scripture will prove this sufficiently to be true. And whether this misery shall not remove (and not till then) when all the branches of mankind shall look upon themselves as one man, and upon the earth as a common Treasury to all, without respecting persons, every one acknowledging the law of righteousnesse in them and over them, and walking in his light purely? then cast away your buying and selling the earth, with her fruits, it is unrighteous, it lifts up one above another, it makes one man oppresse another, and is the burthen of the Creation.

3. Whether the work of restoration lies not in removing covetousnesse, casting that Serpent out of heaven, (mankind) and making man to live in the light of righteousnesse, not in words only, as Preachers do, but in action, whereby the Creation shines in glory? I affirm it.

4. Whether is the King of righteousnesse a *respecter of persons* yea, or no? If you say no, then who makes this difference, that the elder brother shall be lord of the land, and the younger brother a slave and beggar? I affirm, it was and is covetousnesse, since the fall, not the King of righteousnesse before the fall, that made that difference; therefore if you will be Preachers, hold forth the law of righteousnesse purely, and not the confused law of covetousnesse, which is the murtherer: the law of righteousnesse would have every one to injoy the benefit of his creation, that is, to have food and rayment by his labour freely in the land of his nativity, but covetousnesse will

have none to live free, but he that hath the strongest arme of flesh; all others must be servants.

5. Whether a man can have true peace by walking in the Law of covetousnesse and self, as generally all do, or by walking in the Law of universall righteousnesse; doing as he would be done by? I affirm there is no true peace, till men talk lesse, and live more actually in the power of universall righteousnesse. Then you Preachers, lay aside your multitude of words, and your selfish doctrines, for you confound and delude the people.

6. Whether does the King of righteousnesse bid you love or hate your enemies, if you say love them, then I demand of you, why do some of you in your Pulpits, and elsewhere, stir up the people to beat, to imprison, put to death or banish, or not to buy and sell with those that endeavour to restore the earth to a common treasury again? surely at the worst, you can make them but your enemies; therefore love them, win them by love, do not hate them, they do not hate you.

7. Whether it be not a great breach of the Nationall Covenant, to give two sorts of people their freedom, that is, Gentry and Clergy, and deny it to the rest? I affirm it is a high breach, for mans Laws makes these two sorts of people, the Antichristian task-masters over the common people. The one forcing the people to give them rent for the earth, and to work for hire for them. The other which is the Clergy, that force a maintenance of tithes from the people;[2] a practise which Christ, the Apostles and Prophets never walked in; therefore surely you are the false Christs, and false Prophets, that are risen up in these latter daies.

Thus I have declared to you, and to all in the whole world, what that power of life is, that is in me. And knowing that the Spirit of righteousnesse does appear in many in this Land, I desire all of you seriously in love and humility, to consider of this businesse of publike community, which I am carried forth in the power of love, and clear light of universall righteousnesse, to advance as much as I can; and I can do no other, the Law of love in my heart does so constrain me, by reason whereof I am called fool, mad man, and have many slanderous reports cast upon me, and meet with much fury from some covetous people, under all which my spirit is made patient, & is guarded with joy and peace: I hate none, I love all, I delight to see every one live comfortably. I would have none live in poverty, straits or sorrows; therefore if you find any selfishnesse in this work, or discover any thing that is destructive to the whole Creation, that you would open your hearts as freely to me in declaring my weaknesse to me, as I have been open-hearted in declaring that which I find and feel much life and strength in. But if you see righteousnesse in it, and that it holds forth the strength of universall love to all without respect to persons, so that our Creator is honored in the work of his hand, then own it, and justifie it, and let the power of love have his freedom and glory.

Jerrard Winstanly.

The Reformation that England now is to endeavour, is not to remove the Norman *Yoke* only, and to bring us back to be governed by those Laws that were before *William the Conqueror* came in, as if that were the rule or mark we aime at: No, that is not it; but the Reformation is according to the Word of God, and that is the pure Law of righteousnesse before the fall, which made all things, unto which all things are to be restored: and he that endeavours not that, is a Covenant-breaker.

This Letter with the Questions were delivered by the Authors own hand to the Generall, and the chief Officers, and they very mildly promised they would read it, and consider of it.

FINIS.

NOTES

1. The Council of State had alerted Fairfax to the 'disorderly and tumultuous' Diggers on 16 April 1649. Winstanley and Everard gained an audience with the Lord General in Whitehall on 20 April. Fairfax then visited St George's Hill on 30 May, en route to London after putting down the Leveller mutiny at Burford.

2. Tithes extracted one tenth of parishioners' produce or earnings for the benefit of the local clergyman – or the local lord, given that many tithes had been impropriated.

A

WATCH-WORD
TO

The City of London,

AND THE

ARMIE:

WHEREIN

You may see that Englands freedome, which
should be the result of all our Victories, is sinking deeper
under the Norman power, as appears by this relation of the
unrighteous proceedings of Kingstone-Court against some of
the Diggers at *George*-hill, under colour of Law; but yet
thereby the cause of the Diggers is more brightened and
strengthened: so that every one singly may truly say what his
freedome is, and where it lies.[1]

By *Jerrard Winstanly*.

When these clay-bodies are in grave, and children stand in place,
This shews we stood for truth and peace, and freedom in our daies;
And true born sons we shall appear of England that's our mother,
No Priests nor Lawyers wiles t'imbrace, their slavery wee'l discover.

L O N D O N,
Printed for *Giles Calvert* at the Sign of the black
Spread-Eagle, at the West end of *Pauls*, 1 6 4 9.

TO THE CITY OF *LONDON*, FREEDOME AND PEACE DESIRED.

Thou City of London, I am one of thy sons by freedome,[2] and I do truly love thy peace; while I had an estate in thee, I was free to offer my Mite into thy publike Treasury Guild-hall, for a preservation to thee, and the whole Land; but by thy cheating sons in the theeving art of buying and selling, and by the burdens of, and for the Souldiery in the beginning of the war, I was beaten out both of estate and trade, and forced to accept of the good will of friends crediting of me, to live a Countrey-life, and there likewise by the burthen of Taxes and much Free-quarter, my weak back found the burthen heavier then I could bear; yet in all the passages of these eight yeers troubles I have been willing to lay out what my Talent was, to procure Englands peace inward and outward, and yet all along I have found such as in words have professed the same cause, to be enemies to me. Not a full yeere since, being quiet at my work, my heart was filled with sweet thoughts, and many things were revealed to me which I never read in books, nor heard from the mouth of any flesh, and when I began to speak of them, some people could not bear my words, and amongst those revelations this was one, *That the earth shall be made a common Treasury of livelihood to whole mankind, without respect of persons*; and I had a voice within me bad me declare it all abroad, which I did obey, for I declared it by word of mouth wheresoever I came, then I was made to write a little book called, *The new Law of righteousness*, and therein I declared it; yet my mind was not at rest, because nothing was acted, and thoughts run in me, that words and writings were all nothing, and must die, for action is the life of all, and if thou dost not act, thou dost nothing. Within a little time I was made obedient to the word in that particular likewise; for I tooke my spade and went and broke the ground upon *George-hill* in Surrey, thereby declaring freedome to the Creation, and that the earth must be set free from intanglements of Lords and Landlords, and that it shall become a common Treasury to all, as it was first made and given to the sonnes of men: For which doing the Dragon presently casts a flood of water to drown the manchild, even that freedom that now is declared, for the old Norman Prerogative Lord of that Mannour M *Drake*,[3] caused me to be arrested for a trespasse against him, in digging upon that barren Heath, and the unrighteous proceedings of Kingstone Court in this businesse I have here declared to thee, and to the whole land, that you may consider the case that England is in; all men have stood for freedom, thou hast kept fasting daies, and prayed in morning exercises for freedom; thou hast given thanks for victories, because hopes of freedome; plentie of Petitions and promises thereupon have been made for freedome, and now the common enemy is gone, you are all like men in a mist, seeking for freedom, and know not where, nor what it is: and those of the richer sort of you that see it, are ashamed and afraid to owne it, because it comes clothed in a clownish garment, and open to the best language that scoffing *Ishmael* can afford, or that railing *Rabsheka* can speak, or furious *Pharoah* can act against him; for freedom is the man that will turn the world upside downe, therefore no wonder he hath enemies.

And assure your selves, if you pitch not right now upon the right point of freedome in action, as your Covenant hath it in words, you will wrap up your children in greater slavery then ever you were in: the Word of God is Love, and when all thy actions are done in love to the whole Creation, then thou advancest freedome, and freedome is Christ in you, and Christ among you; bondage is Satan in you, and Satan among you: no true freedom can be established for Englands peace, or prove you faithfull in Covenant, but such a one as hath respect to the poor, as well as the rich; for if thou consent to freedom to the rich in the City and givest freedome to the Free-holders in the Countrey, and to Priests and Lawyers, and Lords of Mannours and Impropriators, and yet allowest the poor no freedome, thou art then a declared hypocrite, and all thy prayers, fasts, and thanksgivings are, and will be proved an abomination to the Lord, and freedome himselfe will be the poors portion, when thou shalt lie groaning in bondage.

I have declared this truth to the Army and Parliament,[4] and now I have declared it to thee likewise, that none of you that are the fleshly strength of this Land may be left without excuse, for now you have been all spoken to, and because I have obeyed the voice of the Lord in this thing, therefore doe the Free-holders and Lords of Mannours seek to oppresse me in the outward livelihood of the world, but I am in peace. And London, nay England look to thy freedom, I'le assure thee, thou art very neere to be cheated of it, and if thou lose it now after all thy boasting, truly thy posterity will curse thee, for thy unfaithfulnesse to them: every one talks of freedome, but there are but few that act for freedome, and the actors for freedome are oppressed by the talkers and verball professors of freedome; if thou wouldst know what true freedome is, read over this and other my writings, and thou shalt see it lies in the community in spirit, and community in the earthly treasury, and this is Christ the true manchild spread abroad in the Creation, restoring all things into himselfe; and so I leave thee,

August 26. 1649.

Being a free Denizon of thee, and a true
lover of thy peace,

Jerrard Winstanly.

A WATCH-WORD TO THE CITY OF LONDON, AND THE ARMY.

Whereas we *Henry Bickarstaffe, Thomas Star,* and *Jerrard Winstanly,* were arrested into Kingstone Court, by *Thomas Wenman, Ralph Verney,* and *Richard Winwood,*[5] for a trespasse in digging upon George-hill in Surrey, being the rights of Mr. *Drake* the Lord of that Mannour, as they say, we all three did appear the first Court day of our arrest, and demanded of the Court, what was laid to our Charge, and to give answer thereunto our selves: But the answer of your Court was this, that you would not tell us what the Trespasse was, unlesse we would fee an Attorney to speak for us; we told them we were to plead our own cause, for we knew no Lawyer that we could trust with this businesse: we desired a copie of the Declaration, and profered to pay for it; and still you denied us, unlesse we would fee an Attorney. But in conclusion, the Recorder of your Court told us, the cause was not entred; we appeared two Court daies after this, and desired to see the Declaration, and still you denied us, unlesse we will fee an Attorney; so greedy are these Attorneys after money, more then to justifie a righteous cause: we told them we could not fee any, unlesse we would willfully break our Nationall Covenant, which both Parliament and people have taken joyntly together to endeavour a Reformation. And unlesse we would be professed Traytors to this Nation and Common-wealth of England, by upholding the old Norman tyrannicall and destructive Lawes, when they are to be cast out of equity, and reason be the Moderator.

Then seeing you would not suffer us to speak, one of us brought the following writing into your Court, that you might read our answer; because we would acknowledge all righteous proceedings in Law, though some slander us, and say we deny all Law, because we deny the corruption in Law, and endeavour a Reformation in our place and calling, according to that Nationall Covenant: and we know if your Lawes be built upon equity and reason, you ought both to have heard us speak, and read our answer; for that is no righteous Law, whereby to keep a Common-wealth in peace, when one sort shall be suffered to speak, and not another, as you deal with us, to passe sentence and execution upon us, before both sides be heard to speak.

This principle in the forehead of your Laws, foretells destruction to this Common-wealth: for it declares that the Laws that follow such refusall, are selfish and theevish, and full of murder, protecting all that get money by their Laws, and crushing all others.

The writer hereof does require Mr. *Drake*, as he is a Parliamentman; therefore a man counted able to speak rationally, to plead this cause of digging with me, and if he shew a just and rationall title that Lords of Mannours have to the Commons, and that they have a just power from God, to call it their right, shutting out others; then I will write as much against it, as ever I writ for this cause. But if I shew by the Law of Righteousnesse, that the poorest man hath as true a title and just right to the Land, as the richest man, and that undeniably the earth ought to be a common treasury of livelihood for all, without respecting persons: Then I shall require no more of Mr. *Drake*, but that he would justifie our cause of digging, and declare abroad, that the Commons ought to be free to all sorts, and that it is a great trespasse before the Lord God Almighty, for one to hinder another of his liberty to dig the earth, that he might feed and cloath himself with the fruits of his labor therefrom freely, without owning any Landlord, or paying any rent to any person of his own kind.

I sent this following answer to the Arrest, in writing into Kingstone Court: In foure passages, your Court hath gone contrary to the righteousnesse of your own Statute Laws: For first it is mentioned in 36. *Ed*. 3. 15. that no Processe, Warrant, or Arrest should be served, till after the cause was recorded and entred;[6] but your Bailiffe either could not, or would not tell us the cause when he arrested us, and Mr. *Rogers* your Recorder told us the first Court day we appeared, that our cause was not entred.

Secondly, we appeared two other Court daies, and desired a copy of the Declaration, and profered to pay for it, and you denied us. This is contrary to equity and reason, which is the foundation your Lawes are, or should be built upon, if you would have England to be a Common-wealth, and stand in peace.

Thirdly, we desired to plead our own cause, and you denied us, but told us we must fee an Attorney to speak for us, or els you would mark us for default in not appearance. This is contrary to your own Laws likewise, for in 28. *Ed.* 1. 11. chap. there is freedome given to a man to speak for himself, or els he may choose his father, friend or neighbour to plead for him, without the help of any other Lawyer.[7]

Fourthly, you have granted a judgement against us, and are proceeding to an execution, and this is contrary likewise to your own Laws, which say, that no plaint ought to be received, or judgement passed, till the cause be heard, and witnesses present, to testifie the plaint to be true, as Sir *Edward Cook 2. part of Institutes* upon the 29. chap. of *Magna Charta*, fol. 51. 52. 53. The *Mirror of Justice*.[8]

But that all men may see, we are neither ashamed nor afraid, to justifie that cause we are arrested for, neither to refuse to answer to it in a righteous way, therefore we have here delivered this up in writing, and we leave it in your hands, disavowing the proceedings of your Court, because you uphold Prerogative oppression, though the Kingly office be taken away, and the Parliament hath declared England a Common-Wealth,[9] so that Prerogative Laws cannot be in force, unlesse you be besotted by your covetousnesse and envy.

We deny that we have trespassed against those three men, or Mr. *Drake* either, or that we should trespasse against any, if we should dig up, or plow for a livelihood, upon any the wast

Land in England; for thereby we break no particular Law made by any Act of Parliament, but only an ancient custome, bred in the strength of Kingly Prerogative, which is that old Law or custome, by which Lords of Mannours lay claime to the Commons, which is of no force now to bind the people of England, since the Kingly power and office was cast out: and the common people, who have cast out the oppressor, by their purse and person, have not authorized any as yet, to give away from them their purchased freedome; and if any assume a power to give away, or withhold this purchased freedome, they are Traytors to this Common-Wealth of England: and if they imprison, oppresse, or put to death any for standing to maintaine the purchased freedome, they are murderers and thieves, and no just rulers.

Therefore in the light of reason and equity, and in the light of the Nationall Covenant, which Parliament and people have taken, with joynt consent: all such Prerogative customes, which by experience we have found to burden the Nation, ought to be cast out, with the Kingly office, and the Land of England now ought to be a free Land, and a common treasury to all her children, otherwise it cannot properly be called a Common-Wealth.

Therefore we justifie our act of digging upon that hill, to make the earth a common treasurie. First, because the earth was made by Almighty God, to be a common treasury of livelihood for whole mankind in all his branches, without respect of persons; and that not any one according to the Word of God (which is love) the pure Law of righteousnesse, ought to be Lord or landlord over another, but whole mankind was made equall, and knit into one body by one spirit of love, which is Christ in you the hope of glory, even all the members of mans body, called the little world, are united into equality of love, to preserve the whole body.

But since the fall of man there from, which came in by the rising up of covetousnesse in the heart of mankind (to which Serpent the man consented) and from thence mankind was called *A-dam*: for this covetousnesse makes mankind to be a stoppage of freedome in the creation, and by this covetous power, one branch of mankind began to lift up himself above another, as *Cain* lifted up himself, and killed his brother *Abel*: and so one branch did kill and steal away the comfortable use of the earth from another, as it is now: the elder brother lives in a continuall theevery, stealing the Land from the younger brother. And the plain truth is, theeves and murderers upheld by preaching witches and deceivers, rule the Nations: and for the present, the Laws and Government of the world, are Laws of darknesse, and the divells Kingdome, for covetousnesse rules all. And the power of the sword over brethren in Armies, in Arrests, in Prisons, in gallows, and in other inferiour torments, inflicted by some upon others, as the oppression of Lords of Mannours, hindring the poore from the use of the common Land, is *Adam* fallen, or *Cain* killing *Abel* to this very day.

And these Prerogative oppressors, are the Adamites & Cainites that walk contrary to the Word of God (which is love) by upholding murder and theft, by Laws which their Fathers made, and which they now justifie; for in the conquests that Kings got, their Ancestors did murder and kill, and steal away the earth, and removed the Land mark from the conquered, and made Laws to imprison, torment, or put to death, all that would adventure to take the Land from them againe, and left both that stoln Land, and murdering Laws to their children, the Lords of Mannours, and Freeholders, who now with violence, do justifie their Fathers wickednesse, by holding fast, that which was left them by succession.

For what are all the Laws of the Nations, in this corrupt covetous Government, lifting up one branch of *Adam* mankind above another, the Conqueror, above the conquered, or those that have power above them that are weak, I say what are they, but Laws of murder and theft, yea enmity it self, against the Law of righteousnesse, which is love, which makes people do, as they would be done unto?

And so all Kingly power, (in one or many mens hands) raigning by the sword, giving the use of the earth to some of mankind (called by him his Gentry) and denying the free use of the Earth to others, called the younger brothers, or common people, is no other but *Cain* lifted up above *Abel*; the Prerogative Lawes is *Belzebub*, for they are the strength of covetousnesse and bondage in the creation, lifting up one, and casting down another: the Atturneyes and Priests, and Lawyers, and Bayliffs are servants to *Belzebub*, and are Devils; their Prisons, Whips, and Gallows are the torments of this Hell, or government of darknesse; for mind it all along, and you shall see, that covetousnesse and bitter envie gets freedome by these Lawes; But the sincere and meek in spirit, is trod under foot.

And this is that power, that hath made such havock in the Creation, it is that murderer and Devill that is to be cast out: this power of covetousnesse, is he that does countenance murder and theft in them that maintaines his Kingdom by the sword of Iron, and punishes it in others: and so that which is called a sin in the Common people, if they act such things, is counted no sin in the action of Kings, because they have the power of the sword in their hands, the fear whereof makes people to feare them.

But since this Kingly Office by the Parliament, is cast out of *England*, and *England* by them is declared to be a free State or Common-wealth, we are in the first place thereby set free from those bonds and ties that the Kings laid upon us: Therefore this Tyranny of one over another, as of Lords of Mannors over the Common people, and for people to be forced to hire Lawyers to plead their causes for them, when they are able to plead themselves, ought to be taken away with the Kingly Office, because they are the strength of the Antient Prerogative custom.

Secondly we justifie our digging upon *George*'s hill to make the Earth a common Treasury, because all sorts of people have lent assistance of purse and person to cast out the Kingly Office, as being a burden *England* groaned under; therefore those from whom money and blood was received, ought to obtain freedom in the Land to themselves and Posterity, by the Law of contract between Parliament and People.

But all sorts, poor as well as rich, Tenant as well as Landlord, have paid Taxes, Free-quarter, Excise, or adventured their lives, to cast out that Kingly Office.

Therefore, all sorts of people ought to have freedom in the Land of this their nativity, without respecting persons, now the Kingly Office is cast out, by their joynt assistance. And those that doe imprison, oppresse and take away the livelihood of those that rise up to take Possession of this purchased freedome, are Traitors to this Nation, and Enemies to righteousnesse: And of this number are those men that have arrested, or that may arrest the Diggers, that endeavour to advance freedom; therefore I say all sorts ought to have their freedom.

And that in regard they have not only joyned persons and purses together, but in regard likewise, they took the Nationall Covenant, with joynt consent together, which the Parliament did make, of whom Mr *Drake* that caused us to be arrested was one; which Covenant likewise, the Ministers in their Sermons, most vehemently prest upon the people to take the intent whereof was this, That every one in his severall place and calling, should endeavor the peace, safety and freedom of *England*, and that the Parliament should assist the people, and the people the Parliament, and every one that had taken it, should assist those that had taken it, while they were in pursuit thereof, as in the sixth Article of the Nationall Covenant.[10]

But now Mr *Drake* that was one that made this Covenant, and the *Surrey* Ministers that took it with great zeal at *Kingstone*, which I was eye witnesse to, and shall be of their hypocrisie therein; have set up a Lecturer at *Cobham* one purpose to drive off the Diggers to forsake the persuit of their Covenant are the most vehement to break Covenant and to hinder them that

would keep it, neither entring into peace themselves, nor suffering them that are entring in to enter.

But in regard some of us did dig upon *George*'s Hill, thereby
to take Possession of that freedom we have recovered out
of the hands of the Kingly Office, and thereby endeavour a
Reformation in our place and calling according to the Word of
God (which is Love:) And while we are in persuit of this our
Covenant, we expect both Parliament that made the Covenant,
and the Officers of this Court, and Parish Ministers, and Lords
of Mannors themselves, and especially Mr *Drake*, to assist us
herein, against all that shall oppose us in this righteous work
of making the Earth a common Treasury; and not to beat us,
imprison us, or take away our estates or lives, unlesse they will
wilfully break Covenant with God and man, to please their own
covetous froward heart, and thereby declare themselves to be
the worst of Devils.

Therefore, in that we doe dig upon that Hill, we do not
thereby take away other mens rights, neither do we demand
of this Court, or from the Parliament, what is theirs and not
ours: But we demand our own to be set free to us and them
out of the Tyrannicall oppression of antient custome of Kingly
Prerogative; and let us have no more gods to rule over us, but
the King of righteousnesse only.

Therefore as the Free-holders claime a quietnesse and freedom in their inclosures, as it is fit they should have, so we that
are younger brothers, or the poore oppressed, we claime our
freedome in the Commons, that so elder and younger brother
may live quietly and in peace, together freed from the straits of
poverty and oppression, in this Land of our nativitie.

Thus we have in writing declared in effect, what we should
say, if we had liberty to speak before you, declaring withall,
that your Court cannot end this Controversie in that equity
and reason of it, which wee stand to maintaine: Therefore we
have appealed to the Parliament, who have received our Appeal

and promised an Answer, and we wait for it;[11] And we leave this with you, and let Reason and righteousnesse be our Iudge; therefore we hope you will do nothing rashly, but seriously consider of this cause before you proceed to execution upon us.

You say God will blast our work, and you say, you are in the right, and we are in the wrong: Now if you be Christians, as you say you are; Then doe you act love to us, as we doe to you; and let both sides waite with patience on the Lord, to see who he blesses; but if you oppose by violence, arrest us, judge, condemn and execute us, and yet will not suffer us to speak for our selves, but you will force us to give money to our Enemies to speak for us, surely you cannot say your cause is right; but hereby you justifie our cause to be right, because you are the Persecutors of a loving meek spirited people, and so declare that the God you say that will blast us, is covetousnesse, whom you serve by your persecuting power.

> *Covetous might may overcome rationall right for a time,*
> *But rationall right must conquer covetous might, and that's the life*
> *of mine.*

> *The Law is righteous, just and good, when Reason is the rule,*
> *But who so rules by the fleshly will, declares himself a foole.*

Well, this same writing was delivered into their Court, but they cast it away and would not read it, and all was because I would not fee an Atturney; and then the next Court day following, before there was any tryall of our cause, for there was none suffered to speak but the Plaintiffe, they passed a Iudgement, and after that an Execution.

Now their Iury was made of rich Free-holders, and such as stand strongly for the Norman power: And though our digging upon that barren Common hath done the Common good, yet this jury brings in damages of ten pounds a man, and the charges of the Plaintiffe in their Court, twenty nine shillings and a peny; and this was their sentence and the passing of the Execution upon us.

And 2 dayes after (for in this case they can end a cause speedily in their Court; but when the Atturney and Lawyer get money they keep a cause depending seven yeares, to the utter undoing of the parties, so unrighteous is the Law, and Lawyers) I say, two dayes after they sent to execute the execution, and they put *Henry Beckarstaffe* in prison, but after three dayes, Mr *Drake* released him again, *Beckarstaffe* not knowing of it till the release came; They seek after *Thomas Star* to imprison his body, who is a poore man not worth ten pounds.

Then they came privately by day to *Gerrard Winstanleys* house, and drove away foure Cowes; I not knowing of it and some of the Lords Tenants rode to the next Town shouting the diggers were conquered, the diggers were conquered. Truly it is an easie thing to beat a man, and cry conquest over him after his hands are tied, as they tyed ours. But if their cause be so good, why will they not suffer us to speak, and let reason and equity, the foundation of righteous Lawes, judge them and us. But strangers made rescue of those Cowes, and drove them astray out of the Bailiffes hands, so that the Bailiffes lost them; but before the Bailiffes had lost the Cowes, I hearing of it went to them and said here is my body, take me that I may come to speak to those *Normans* that have stolne our land from us; and let the Cowes go, for they are none of mine; and after some time, they telling me that they had nothing against my body, it was my goods they were to have; then said I take my goods, for the Cowes are not mine; and so I went away and left them, being quiet in my heart, and filled with comfort within my self, that the King of righteousnesse would cause this to work for the advancing of his own Cause, which I prefer above estate or livelyhood.

Saying within my heart as I went along, that if I could not get meat to eat, I would feed upon bread, milk and cheese; and if they take the Cowes, that I cannot feed on this, or hereby make a breach between me and him that owns the Cowes, then Ile feed upon bread and beere, till the King of righteousnesse clear up my innocency, and the justice of his own cause: and if this be taken from me for maintaining his Cause, Ile stand still and see what he will doe with me, for as yet I know not.

Saying likewise within my heart as I was walking along, O thou King of righteousnesse shew thy power, and do thy work thyself, and free thy people now from under this heavy bondage of miserie, *Pharoah* the covetous power. And the answer in my heart was satisfactory and full of sweet joy and peace: and so I said Father, do what thou wilt, this cause is thine, and thou knowest that the love to righteousnesse makes me do what I do.

I was made to appeal to the Father of life in the speakings of my heart likewise thus: Father thou knowest that what I have writ or spoken, concerning this light, that the earth should be restored and become a common Treasurie for all mankind, without respect of persons, was thy free revelation to me, I never read it in any book, I heard it from no mouth of flesh till I understood it from thy teaching first within me. I did not study nor imagine the conceit of it; self-love to my own particular body does not carry me along in the mannaging of this businesse; but the power of love flowing forth to the liberty and peace of thy whole Creation, to enemies as well as friends: nay towards those that oppresse me, endeavouring to make me a beggar to them. And since I did obey thy voice, to speak and act this truth, I am hated, reproached, and oppressed on evere side. Such as make profession of thee, yet revile me. And though they see I cannot fight with fleshly weapons, yet they will strive with me by that power. And so I see Father, that *England* yet does choose rather to fight with the Sword of Iron, and covetousnesse, then by the Sword of the Spirit which is love: and what thy purpose is with this land, or with my body, I know not; but establish thy power in me, and then do what pleases thee.

These and such like sweet thoughts dwelt upon my heart as I went along, and I feel my self now like a man in a storm, standing under shelter upon a hill in peace, waiting till the storm be over to see the end of it, and of many other things that my eye is fixed upon: But I will let this passe,

And return again to the Dragons Den, or Hornets nest, the selfish murdering fleshly Lawes of this Nation, which hangs some for stealing and protects others in stealing; Lords of Mannours stole the land from their fellow creatures formerly in the conquests of Kings, and now they have made Lawes to imprison and hang all those that seek to recover the land again out of their thieving murdering hands.

They took away the Cowes which were my livelyhood, and beat them with their clubs, that the Cowes heads and sides did swell, which grieved tender hearts to see: and yet these Cowes never were upon *George* Hill, nor never digged upon that ground, and yet the poore beasts must suffer because they gave milk to feed me, but they were driven away out of those Devills hands the Bailiffes, and were delivered out of hell at that time.

And thus Lords of Mannours, their Bailiffes the true upholders of the *Norman* power, and some Freeholders that doe oppose this publick work, are such as the countrey knowes have beene no friends to that Cause the Parliament declared for, but to the Kingly power; and now if they get the foot fast in the stirrup, they will lift themselves again into the *Norman* saddle; and they do it secretly; for they keep up the *Norman* Lawes and thereby Traytours to freedome, get into places of Law and power, and by that will enslave *England* more then it was under the Kingly power.

Therefore *England* beware; thou art in danger of being brought under the *Norman* power more then ever. The King *Charles* that was successour to *William* the Conquerour thou hast cast out: and though thy Parliament have declared against the Kingly office, and cast it out, and proclaimed *England* a Common wealth, that is to be a free land for the liberty and livelyhood of all her children;

Yet *William* the Conquerours Army begins to gather into head againe, and the old *Norman* Prerogative Law is the place of their randezvous: for though their chief Captain *Charles* be gone, yet his Colonells, which are Lords of Mannours, his Councellours and Divines, which are our Lawyers and Priests, his inferiour officers and Souldiers, which are the Freeholders, and Land-lords, all which did steal away our Land from us when they killed and murdered our Fathers in that *Norman* conquest: And the Bailiffes that are slaves to their covetous lusts and all the ignorant bawling women, against our digging for freedome, are the snapsack boyes and the ammunition sluts that follow the *Norman* Camp.

These are all striving to get into a body againe, that they may set up a new *Norman* slaverie over us; and the place of their randezvous, Prerogative power is fenced already about, with a Line of Communication. An act made by a piece of the Parliament to maintain the old Lawes,[12] which if once this camp be fortified in his full strength, it will cost many a sighing heart, and burdened spirit before it be taken.

And this *Norman* Camp are got into so numerous a body already, that they have appointed their Sutlers to drive away the Cowes which were my livelyhood, and some of them would sell to make money of to pay the Atturney, *Gilder*, and Lawyers their fees, for denying the diggers our priviledge to plead our own cause; for as it is clearly seen that if we be suffered to speak we shall batter to pieces all the old Lawes, and prove the maintainers of them hypocrites and Traitours to this Common wealth of *England*, and then the Atturneys and Lawyers Trade goes down, and Lords of Mannours must be reckoned equall to other men. And this covetous flesh and blood cannot endure.

And other of the Cows were to be killed to victuall the Camp, that is, to feed those *Normans*, *Wil Star & Ned Sutton*, both Freeholders[13] & others the snapsack boyes, and ammunition drabs that helped to drive away the Cows that they might be encouraged by a belly full of stoln goods to stick the closer to the businesse another time. Or else the price of these Cowes were to pay for the sack and Tobacco which the *Norman* officers of Knights, Gentlemen, and rich Freeholders did spend at the White Lion at *Cobham*, when they met the 24. of *August* 1649, to advise together what course they should take to subdue the diggers; for say they, if the cause of the diggers stand, we shall lose all our honour and titles, and we that have had the glory of the earth shall be of no more account then those slaves our servants and younger brothers that have been footstools to us and our Fathers ever since the *Norman William* our beloved Generall took this land (not by love) but by a sharp sword, the power by which we stand: and though we own Christ by name, yet we will not do as he did to save enemies, but by our sword we will destroy our enemies, and do we not deserve the price of some of the diggers Cows to pay us for this our good service? And doe not our reverend Ministers tell us that *William* the Conquerour, and the succeeding Kings were Gods annointed? And do not they say that our inclosures which were got by that murdering sword, and given by *William* the Conquerour to our Fathers, and so successivly from them, the land is our inheritance, and that God gave it us, and shall these broken fellows, and beggarly rogues take our rights from us, and have the use of the land equall with us? Thus do these *Norman* Gentlemen comfort their hearts, and support themselves with broken reeds, when they meet together in their Counsels.

But stay you *Norman* Gentlemen, let me put in a word amongst you, doth the murderers sword make any man to be Gods anointed? Surely, Iesus Christ was called Gods annointed not because he conquered with a Sword of iron, but because he conquered by love, and the spirit of patience: therefore your Generall was not Gods annointed, as Christ was.

And then the Earth was not made to be the successive inheritance of children of murderers, that had the strongest arm of flesh, and the best sword, that can tread others under foot with a bold brasen forehead under colour of the Law of justice as the *Norman* power does; But it was made for all by the Law of right-eousnesse, and he gives the whole Earth to be the inheritance of every single branch of mankind without respect of persons, and he that is filled with the love of this righteous King, doing as he would be done by is a true annointed one.

Therefore, that god whom you serve, and which did intitle you Lords, Knights Gentlemen, and Landlords, is covetousnesse, the god of this world, which alwayes was a murderer, a devil and father of lies, under whose dark governing power, both you and all the nations of the world for the present are under. But the King of righteousnesse or God of love whom I serve, did not call the earth your inheritance, shutting out others, but gave the earth to be a common treasurie to whole mankind (who is the Lord of it) without respect of person.

This power of love, is the King of righteousnesse, the Lord God Almighty that rules the whole Creation in peace, that is the Seed that breaks covetousnesse the Serpents head; he is the restoring power, that is now rising up to change all things into his own nature, he will be your Iudge, for vengance is his; and for any wrong you have done me, as I can tell you of many, yet I have given all matters of judgment and vengance into his hand, and I am sure he will doe right, and discover him that is the true Trespasser, that take away my rights from me.

And take notice of this, you Lords of Mannors, and Norman Gentry, though you should kill my body or starve me in prison, yet know, that the more you strive, the more troubles you hearts shall be filled with; and doe the worst you can to hinder publick freedom, you shall come off losers in the later end, I meane you shall lose your Kingdom of darknesse, though I lose my livelihood, the poor Cowes that is my living, and should be imprisoned; you have been told this 12 Months agoe, that you should lose ground by striving, and will you not take warning, will you needs shame your selves, to let the poore Diggers take away your Kingdome from you? surely, the power that is in them, will take the rule and government from you, and give it a people that will make better use of it.

Alas! you poor blind earth mouls, you strive to take away my livelihood, and the liberty of this poor weak frame my body of flesh, which is my house I dwell in for a time; but I strive to cast down your kingdom of darknesse, and to open Hell gates, and to break the Devils bands asunder, wherewith you are tied, that you my Enemies may live in peace, and that is all the harm I would have you to have.

Therefore you Lords of Mannors, you Free-holders, you Norman-Clergy, oppressing Tith-mungers, and you of the Parliament men, that have plaid fast and loose with this poor Nation, for what is past let it goe; hereafter advance freedom and liberty, and pluck up bondage; and sinne no more by Lording it over your Lords and Masters, that set you upon those Parliament Seats, lest worse things befall you then yet hath.

But to return again to Mr *Gilders* advice, the Atturney of *Kingstone* Court, and the proceeding of that Court with the Cowes; you heare how they did judge, condemn and execute me, not suffering me to speak; and though those four Cowes were rescued out of their hands by strangers, not by me; and so by their own Law, they should have looked after the Rescuers, yet contrary to their own Law, they came againe to *Winstanleys* dwelling a fortnight after, and drove away seven Cowes and a Bull in the night time, some of the Cowes being Neighbour's that had hired pasture; and yet the damage which their Norman Iury, and their covetous besotted ignorant Atturney Mr *Gilder*, had judged me to pay for a Trespasse in digging upon that barren *George's* Hill, was but eleven pound nine shillings and a penny charges & all, which they are like never to have of me, for an empty carrier will dance and sing before these Norman theeves and pick-purses: And thus you see they judged and passed sentence upon me but once at their prerogative pleasure, which they call *Englands* Law: but they executed me twice, that they might be sure to kill me. But yet these Cowes likewise are brought home againe, and the heart of my Enemies is put into the pound of vexation because the Cowes are set free. Surely, these Lords of Mannors and the Atturney Mr *Gilder*, that gave advice to Arrest us for digging, have burned their Bibles long agoe, because they have so quite and clean forgotten that Petition in the Lords prayer, *forgive us our trespasses as we forgive them*; for they make this a trespasse against them, for digging upon the wast land of our mother the Land of *England* for a livelihood, when as their Law it self saith, *That the Commons and wasts belong to the poore.*

So that you see the Norman Camp is grown very numerous and big, that they want much beeffe to vituall them, and they are such hungry ones, that they will eat poor lean Cowes, that are little better then skin & bone; and poor Cowes if I keep them in the winter, they are like to be poorer for want of Hay; for before the report of our digging was much known, I bought three Acres of grasse of a Lord of a Mannor, whom I will not here name because I know the councel of others made him prove fals to me; for when the time came to Mow, I brought mony to pay him before hand; but he answered me, I should not have it, but sold it to another before my face; this was because his Parish Priest, and the *Surrey* Ministers, and sorry ones too they are that have set up a Lecture at *Cobham* for a little time, to preach down the Diggers, have bid the people neither to buy nor sell with us, but to beat us, imprison us, or banish us; and thereby they prove themselves to be members of the Beast that had two horns, like a Lamb, and yet speak like a Dragon, & so they fulfill that Scripture in *Rev.* 13.16. *that no man might buy and sell, save he that had the mark of the Beast.* Or else surely, they do it on purpose to quicken us to our work, and to drive us to Plant the Commons with all speed as may be.

But though the Cowes were poor, yet they care not, so the skins will but pay the Lawyers and Atturneys *Gilder* his Fees, and the flesh to feed the snapsack boyes, either to eat and make merry with, or else to sell to make money of, to pay those that drive away the Cowes for their paines or charges they have been at, in this 18 weeks striving to beat the Diggers off their work: But the bones will serve the Bailiffs to pick, because their action will be both proved thievery in stealing another mans cattell, and their trespasse very great against the same man, in opening all the Gates round about the ground, where *Winstanley* dwels, and let Hogs and common Cattell into the standing barly and other corn, which the right owner will seek satisfaction for.

So that the fury of this Norman Camp against the Diggers is so great, that they would not only drive away all the Cowes upon the ground, but spoyl the corn too, and when they had done this mischief, the Bayliffs, & the other Norman snapsack boyes went hollowing and shooting, as if they were dancing at a whitsun Ale; so glad they are to do mischief to the Diggers, that they might hinder the work of freedome.

And why are they so furious against us? but because we endeavour to dig up their Tythes, their Lawyers Fees, their Prisons, and all that Art and Trade of darknesse, whereby they get money under couller of Law; and to plant the plesant fruit trees of freedom, in the room of that cursed thornbush, the power of the murdering sword; so they say, they doe all they do by the Law of the Land which the Parliament hath confirmed to them by an Act: And if so, Then Souldiers where is the price of your blood? and Countrey-men, and Citizens, Where is the price of your Taxes and Free-quarter? If this be the freedom, you are like to have, to be beaten and not be suffered to say why doe you so, and shall have no remedy, unlesse you will Fee a Lawyer (an Enemy) to plead for you, when you are able to plead your own cause better your self, and save that charge, and have your cause ended sooner and with more peace and quietnesse.

And you zealous Preachers, and professors of the City of *London* and you great Officers and Souldiery of the Army,

Where are all your Victories over the Cavaliers, that you made such a blaze in the Land, in giving God thanks for, and which you begged in your Fasting dayes, and morning Exercises; Are they all sunck into the Norman power again, and must the old Prerogative Laws stand; what freedom then did you give thanks for? Surely, that you had killed him that rid upon you, that you may get up into his saddle to ride upon others; O thou City, thou Hypocriticall City! thou blindfold drowsie *England*, that sleps and snores in the bed of covetousnesse, awake, awake, the Enemies is upon thy back, he is ready to scale the walls and enter Possession, and wilt thou not look out.

Does not the streames of bondage run in the same river that it did, and with a bigger stream of Norman power; so that if you awaken not betimes, the flood of Norman Prerogative power, will drown you all; here's more rivers comes into the maine stream, since the storm fell and the waters of fury rises very high, banked in by Laws; and while you are talking and disputing about words, the Norman Souldiers are secretly working among you to advance their power again; and so will take away the benefit of all your victories by a subtle act of intricate Lawes, which the sword in the field could not do against you: and when you have lost that freedom, which you boasted of that you will leave to your posterity, then who must give thanks, you that vapoured in words, or they that lay close in action, waiting to trip up your heels by policy, when the sword could not do it.

I tell thee thou *England*, thy battells now are all spirituall. Dragon against the Lamb, and the power of love against the power of covetousnesse; therefore all that will be Souldiers for Christ, the Law of righteousnesse joyn to the Lamb. He that takes the iron sword now shall perish with it, and would you be a strong Land and flourish in beauty, then fight the Lambs battels, and his strength shall be thy walls and bulwarks.

You Knights, Gentlemen, and Freeholders, that sat in councell at the white Lion in *Cobham* to find out who are our backers, and who stirs us up to dig the Commons, Ile tel you plainly who it is, it is love, the King of righteousnes ruling in our hearts, that makes us thus to act that the creation may be set at liberty, and now I have answered your inquirie, do what you can to him and us his servants: And we require you in his name, to let our cause have a publick triall, and do not work any longer in darknesse, set not your Bailiffes and slaves to come by night to steal away the Cowes of poore men under colour of justice, when as the cause was never yet heard in open Court.

He that backs you; and that sets you to work, to deny to us our younger brother the use of the common land, is covetous-nesse, which is Beelzebub the greatest devill so that there is the 2 generalls known, which you & we fight under, the 2 great Princes of light and darknes, bondage and freedom, that does Act all flesh in the great controversies of the world. These are the 2 men that stir in this busines, that is, the wicked man that councels, & backs you to be so envious and furious against us, and the righteous man Christ, that backs and councells us to love you our enemies. And do we not see that *Gebal, Ammon* and *Amaleck,* and all the rabble of the nations, Lords, Knights, Gentlemen, Lawyers, Bailiffes, Priests, and all the *Norman* snap-sack boyes, and ammunition women to the old *Norman* Camp do all combine together in the art of unrighteous fury, to drive the poore diggers off from their work, that the name of com-munity and freedome which is Christ, may not be known in earth. Thus I have dealt plainly with you all, and I have not flat-tered Parliament, Army, City, nor Countrey, but have declared in this, and other writings the whole light of that truth revealed to me by the word of the Lord and I shall now wait to see his hand to do his own work in what time, and by what instru-ments he pleases. And I see the poore must first be picked out, and honoured in this work, for they begin to receive the word of righteousnesse, but the rich generally are enemies to true freedome.

The work of digging still goes on, and stops not for a rest;
The cowes were gone, but are return'd, and we are all at rest.
No money's paid, nor n'ver shall, to Lawyer or his man
To plead our cause, for therein wee'll do the best we can.
In Cobham *on the little Heath our digging there goes on.*
And all our friends they live in love, as if they were but one.

Thus you Gentlemen, that will have no Law to rule over you, but your Prerogative will must be above Law, and above us that are the younger brother in the Land; but if you say, no, your wil shal be subject to Law: then I demand of you Mr *Drake*, Mr *Gilder*, and other the Bailiffes and Officers of *Kingston* Court, why will you arrest us, and trouble us, and say we trespasse against you, and though we came to answer to your arrest, and to plead our own cause, yet contrary to the equity, nay contrary to the bare letter that the Law, as I shewed you before, you denyed me that priviledge, but went on and did condemne and execute a force-able power upon body and goods, is not your will here, above Law? do you not hereby uphold the *Norman* conquest?

Mr *Drake*, you are a Parliament man, and was not the begin-ning of the quarrel between King *Charles* and your House? This the King pleaded to uphold Prerogative, and you were against it, and yet must a Parliament man be the first man to uphold Prerogative, who are but servants to the Nation for the peace and liberty of every one, not conquering Kings to make their wil a Law? did you not promise liberty to the whole Nation, in case the Cavalier party were cast out? and why now wil you seek liberty to your self and Gentry, with the deniall of just liberty and freedome to the common people, that have born the greatest burden?

You have arrested us for digging upon the common Land, you have executed your unrighteous power, in distraining cattel, imprisoning our bodies, and yet our cause was never publickly heard, neither can it be proved that we have broke any Law, that is built upon equity and reason, therefore we wonder where you had your power to rule over us by will, more than we to rule over you by our will. We request you before you go too far, not to let covetousnesse be your Master, trample not others under your feet, under colour of Law, as if none knew equity of Law but you; for me and our estates shall be horns in your eyes, and pricks in your sides, and you may curse that Councell bid you beg our estates, or imprison our persons. But this we request that you would let us have a fair open triall, and do not carry on the course of Law in secret, like *Nicodemus* that is afraid to have his businesse come to light; therefore I challenge you once more, seeing you professe your selves Christians, to let us be brought to a trial of our cause; let your ministers plead with us in the scriptures, & let your Lawyers plead with us in the equity & reason of your own Law; and if you prove us transgressours, then we shal lay down our work and acknowledge we have trespassed against you in digging upon the Commons, & then punish us. But if we prove by Scripture & reason that undeniably the land belongs to one as well as another, then you shal own our work, justifie our cause, & declare that you have done wrong to Christ, who you say is your Lord and master, in abusing us his servants, & your fellow creatures, while we are doing his work. Therefore I knowing you to be men of moderation in outward shew, I desire that your actions towards your fellow creatures may not be like one beast to another, but carry your selves, like man to man; for your proceeding in your pretence of law hitherto against us, is both unrighteous, beastly & divelish, and nothing of the spirit of man seen in it. You Atturnies and Lawyers, you say you are ministers of justice, & we know that equity and reason is, or ought to be the foundation of Law; if so, then plead not for mony altogether but stand for universall justice & equity, then you will have peace; otherwise both you with the corrupt Clergy will be cast out as unsavoury salt.

FINIS.

NOTES

1. Several Diggers including Winstanley were indicted for trespass on 23 June 1649. This document is dated 26 August, by which time the Digger colony had re-located to nearby Cobham – 'our digging there goes on', says Winstanley.

2. Winstanley became a freeman of the Merchant Taylors Company in 1638.

3. Francis Drake of Walton, who sat in the Long Parliament until the purge of December 1648.

4. In addition to their recent dialogue with Fairfax, the Diggers had published *An Appeal to the House of Commons* on 11 July 1649. A Digger petition followed on 24 July. One news-sheet commented that alas, 'the House were upon other weighty affairs when the petition was presented'.

5. Wenman, Verney and Winwood were landowners in Buckinghamshire and Oxfordshire, the first two with family connections to Drake. Why they brought the suit instead of Drake is not known; Sabine (p. 320n) speculates they were trustees for the property under a marriage settlement.

6. The statute cited is from 1362. It required that all legal proceedings be conducted in English rather than French, and entered in Latin. Winstanley may have in mind a later statute of 1368 which stipulated: 'no man be put to answer [an accusation] without presentment [i.e. formal presentation of information] before Justices, or matter of record, or by due process and writ original' (42 Ed. 3. c. 3).

7. Winstanley alights on a statute from 1300 concerned with 'maintenance', i.e. the offence of aiding a party in a legal action without lawful cause (*OED*). The statute ends by clarifying: 'It may not be understood hereby, that any person shall be prohibit to have counsel of pleaders, or of learned men in the law for his fee, or of his parents and next friends.'

8. Sir Edward Coke (1552–1634), Lord Chief Justice and champion of the common law as a constraint on the royal prerogative. The Second Part of his *Institutes* was suppressed until 1641. Coke quoted from *The Mirror of Justices*, a thirteenth-century legal treatise. An English translation of the French original was published in 1646.

9. By Act of Parliament on 19 May 1649, two months after the abolition of the monarchy.

10. According to the sixth Article, 'We shall also . . . in this common cause of religion, liberty and peace of the kingdom, assist and defend all those that enter into this league and covenant.'

11. See n4.

12. Thought to refer to the Act of 17 February 1649 for the smooth continuation of legal proceedings, no longer in the King's name but by authority of Parliament.

13. Corns, et al. (vol. ii, pp. 452–3) describe William Star as a prosperous Walton sheep farmer and Ned Sutton as lessee of the *White Lion* pub mentioned in the text.

A New-yeers Gift
FOR THE

PARLIAMENT
AND
ARMIE:

SHEWING,

What the KINGLY *Power is*;
And that the CAUSE of those
They call

DIGGERS

Is the life and marrow of that Cause the Parliament
hath Declared for, and the Army Fought for;

The perfecting of which Work, will prove *England*
to be the first of Nations, or the tenth part of the city
Babylon,
that fals off from the Beast first, and that sets the Crown
upon Christs head, to govern the World in
Righteousness:

By *Jerrard Winstanley* a lover of *Englands* freedom and
Peace.[1]

Die Pride and Envie; Flesh, take the poor's advice.
Covetousnesse be gon: Come, Truth and Love arise.
Patience take the Crown; throw Anger out of dores:
Cast out Hypocrisie and Lust, which follows whores:
Then England *sit in rest; Thy sorrows will have end;*
Thy Sons will live in peace, and each will be a friend.

London, Printed for *Giles Calvert*, 1650.

A NEW YEERS GIFT SENT TO THE PARLIAMENT AND ARMIE.

Gentlemen of the Parliament and Armie; you and the Common people have assisted each other, to cast out the Head of oppression which was Kingly power, seated in one mans hand, and that work is now done, and till that work was done you called upon the people to assist you to deliver this distressed bleeding dying nation out of bondage; And the people came and failed you not, counting neither purse nor blood too dear to part with to effect this work.

The Parliament after this have made an Act to cast out Kingly power, and to make *England* a free Common-wealth. These Acts the People are much rejoyced with, as being words forerunning their freedome, and they wait for their accomplishment that their joy may be full; for as words without action are a cheat, and kills the comfort of a righteous spirit, so words performed in action does comfort and nourish the life thereof.

Now Sirs, wheresoever we spie out Kingly power, no man I hope shall be troubled to declare it, nor afraid to cast it out, having both Act of Parliament, the Souldiers Oath,[2] and the common peoples consent on his side; for Kingly power is like a great spread tree, if you lop the head or top-bow, and let the other Branches and root stand, it will grow again and recover fresher strength.

If any ask me, What Kingly power is? I Answer, there is a twofold Kingly power. The one is, The Kingly power of right-eousnesse, and this is the power of Almightie God, ruling the whole creation in peace, and keeping it together. And this is the power of universall love, leading people into all truth, teach-ing every one to doe as he would be done unto. Now once more striving with flesh and blood, shaking down every thing that cannot stand, and bringing every one into the Unitie of himself, the one Spirit of love and righteousnesse, and so will work a through restauration. But this Kingly power is above all, and will tread all covetousness, pride, envy, and self-love, and all other enemies whatsoever, under his feet, and take the kingdom and government of the Creation out of the hand of self-seeking and self-honouring Flesh, and rule the alone King of Righteousness in the earth; and this indeed is Christ himself, who will cast out the curse; But this is not that Kingly power intended by that Act of Parliament to be cast out, but pretended to be set up, though this Kingly power be much fought against both by Parliament, Armie, Clergy, and people; but when they are made to see him, then they shall mourn, because they have persecuted him.

But the other Kingly power, is the power of unrighteousness, which indeed is the Devil; And O that there were such a heart in Parliament and Army, as to perform your own Act; then People would never complain of you for breach of Covenant, for your Covetousness, Pride, and too much Self-seeking that is in you. And you on the other-side would never have cause to complain of the Peoples murmurings against you. Truly this jarring that is between you and the People is, The Kingly Power; yea that very Kingly power which you have made an Act to cast out; therefore see it be fulfilled on your part; for the Kingly power of Righteousness expects it, or else he will cast you out for Hypocrites and unsavory Salt; for he looks upon all your Actions, and truly there is abundance of Rust about your Actings, which makes them that they do not shine bright.

This Kingly power, is covetousness in his branches, or the power of self-love, ruling in one or in many men over others, and enslaving those who in the Creation are their equals; nay, who are in the strictness of equity rather their Masters: And this Kingly power is usually set in the Chair of Government, under the name of Prerogative, when he rules in one, over other: And under the name of State Priviledge of Parliament, when he rules in many over others: and this Kingly power, is alwayes raised up, and established by the Sword, and therefore he is called the Murderer, or the great red Dragon, which fights against *Michael*, for he enslaves the weakness of the People under him, deny-ing an equal freedom in the Earth to every one, which the Law of Righteousness gave every man in his creation. This I say is Kingly power under darkness, and as he rules in men, so he makes men jar one against another, and is the cause of all Wars and Complainings; he is known by his outward actions, and his action at this very day fills all places; for this power of darkness rules, and would rule, and is that only Enemy that fights against Creation and National Freedom: And this Kingly power is he, which you have made an Act of Parliament to cast out. And now you Rulers of *England*, play the men, and be valiant for the Truth, which is Christ: for assure your selves God will not be mocked, nor the Devil will not be mocked; for First you say and profess you own the Scriptures of Prophets and Apostles, and God looks that you should perform that Word in action: Secondly you have Declared against the Devil, and if you do not now go through with your work, but slack your hand by hypocritical self-love, and so suffer this dark Kingly power to rise higher and Rule, you shall find, he will maule both you, and yours to purpose.

The life of this dark Kingly power, which you have made an Act of Parliament and Oath to cast out, if you search it to the bottom, you shall see it lies within the iron chest of cursed Covetousness, who gives the Earth to some part of mankind, and denies it to another part of mankind: and that part that hath the Earth, hath no right from the Law of creation to take it to himself, and shut out others; but he took it away violently by Theft and Murder in Conquest: As when our Norman *William* came into *England* and conquered, he turned the English out, and gave the Land unto his Norman Souldiers every man his parcel to inclose, and hence rose up Propriety; for this is the fruit of War from the beginning, for it removes Propriety out of a weaker into a stronger hand, but still upholds the curse of Bondage; and hereby the Kingly power which you have made an Act, and Sworn to cast out, does remove himself from one chair to another; and so long as the Sword rules over brethren, (mind what I say) so long the Kingly power of darkness Rules, and so large as yet is his Kingdom; which spreads from Sea to Sea, and fills the Earth; but Christ is rising who will take the Dominion and Kingdom out of his hand, and his power of Righteousness, shall rise and spred from East to West, from North to South, and fill the Earth with himself, and cast the other cursed power out, when Covetousness sheaths his Sword, and ceases to rage in the field; he first makes sharp Laws of Bondage, That those that are conquered, and that by him are appointed not to enjoy the Earth, but are turned out, shall be Servants, Slaves, and Vassals to the Conquerers party: so those Laws that upholds Whips, Prisons, Gallows is but the same power of the Sword that raged, and that was drunk with Blood in the field.

King *Charles*, it is true, was the Head of this Kingly power in *England*, and he Reigned as he was a Successor of the last Norman Conquerer: and whosoever you be, that hath Propriety of Land, hath your Titles and Evidences made to you in his or his Ancestors Name, and from his and their Will and Kingly power; I am sure, he was not our Creator, and therefore parcelled out the Earth to some, and denied it to others, therefore he must needs stand as a Conquerer, and was the Head of this Kingly power, that burdens and oppresses the People, and that is the cause of all our Wars and Divisions; for if this Kingly power of Covetousness, which is the unrighteous Divider, did not yet Rule: both Parliament, Army, and rich People, would cheerfully give consent that those we call Poor should Dig and freely Plant the Waste and Common Land for a livelihood, seeing there is Land enough, and more by half then is made use of, and not be suffered to perish for want. And yet O ye Rulers of *England*, you make a blazing profession, That you know, and that you own God, Christ, and the Scriptures: but did Christ ever declare such hardness of heart? did not he bid the rich man go and sell all that he hath and give to the Poor? and does not the Scripture say, If thou makest a Covenant, keep it, though it be to thy loss: But truly it will not be to your loss, to let your fellow Creatures, your equals in the Creation, nay those that have been faithful in your Cause, and so your Friends; I say it will not be to your loss to let them quietly improve the Waste and Common Land, that they may live in peace, freed from the heavie burdens of Poverty; for hereby our own Land will be increased with all sorts of Commodities, and the People will be knit together in love, to keep out a forreign Enemy that endeavours, and that will endeavour as yet, to come like an Army of cursed Ratts and Mice to destroy our inheritance; so that if this Freedom be quietly granted to us, you grant it but to your selves, to English-men, to your own flesh and blood: and you do but give us our own neither, which Covetousness, in the Kingly power hath, and yet does hold from us; for the Earth in the first Creation of it, was freely given to whole mankind, without respect of Persons; therefore you Lords of mannors, and you Rulers of *England*, if you own God, Christ and Scripture, now make Restitution, and deliver us quiet possession of our Land, which the Kingly power as yet holds from us.

While this Kingly power raigned in one man called *Charls*, all sorts of people complained of oppression, both Gentrie and Common people, because their lands, Inclosures, and Copie-holds were intangled, and because their Trades were destroyed by Monopolizing Patentees, and your troubles were that you could not live free from oppression in the earth: Thereupon you that were the Gentrie, when you were assembled in Parliament, you called upon the poor Common People to come and help you, and cast out oppression; and you that complained are helped and freed, and that top-bow is lopped off the tree of Tyrannie, and Kingly power in that one particular is cast out; but alas oppression is a great tree still, and keeps off the son of freedome from the poor Commons still, he hath many branches and great roots which must be grub'd up, before every one can sing Sions songs in peace.

As we spie out Kingly power we must declare it, and cast it out, or else we shall deny the Parliament of *England* and their Acts, and so prove Traitors to the Land, by denying obedience there-unto. Now there are Three Branches more of Kinglie power greater then the former that oppresses this Land wonderfully; and these are the power of the Tithing Priests over the Tenths of our labours; and the power of Lords of Mannors, holding the free use of the Commons, and wast Land from the poor, and the intolerable oppression either of bad Laws, or of bad Judges cor-rupting good Laws; these are branches of the Norman conquest and Kingly power still, and wants a Reformation.

For as the first, *William* the Conqueror promised, That if the Clergie would preach him up, so that the people might be bewitched, so as to receive him to be Gods Anointed over them, he would give them the Tenths of the Lands increase yeerly; and they did it, and he made good his Promise; and do we not yet see, That if the Clergie can get Tithes or Money, they will turn as the Ruling power turns, any way; to Popery, to Protestantisme; for a King, against a King, for Monarchy, for

State-Government; they cry who bids most wages, they will be on the strongest side, for an Earthly maintenance; yea, and when they are lifted up, they would Rule too, because they are called Spiritual men: It is true indeed, they are spiritual; but it is of the spiritual power of Covetousness and Pride; for the spiritual power of Love and Righteousness they know not; for if they knew it, they would not persecute and raile against him as they do.

The Clergie will serve on any side, like our ancient Laws, that will serve any Master: They will serve the Papists, they will serve the Protestants, they will serve the King, they will serve the States; they are one and the same Tools for Lawyers to work with under any Government. O you Parliament-men of *England*, cast those whorish Laws out of doors, that are so Common, that pretend love to every one, and is faithful to none; for truly, he that goes to Law, as the Proverb is, shall die a Beggar: so that old Whores, and old Laws, picks mens pockets, and undoes them: If the fault lie in the Laws, and much does, burn all your old Law-Books in *Cheapside*, & set up a Government upon your own Foundation: do not put new Wine into old Bottles; but as your Government must be new, so let the Laws be new, or else you will run farther into the Mud, where you stick already, as though you were fast in an *Irish* Bogge; for you are so far sunke, that he must have good eyes that can see where you are: but yet all are not blind, there are eyes that sees you: but if the fault lies in the Judges of the Law, surely such men deserve no power in a Reforming Common-wealth, that burdens all sorts of People.

And truly Ile tell you plain, your Two Acts of Parliament are excellent and Righteous: The One to cast out Kingly power; The Other to make *England* a Free Common-wealth: build upon these Two, it is a firm Foundation, and your House will be the glory of the World; and I am confident, the righteous Spirit will love you: do not stick in the Bogge of covetous-ness; Let not self-love so be-muddy your brain, that you should lose your selves in the thicket of bramble bush-words, and set never a strong Oak of some stable Action for the Freedome of the poor Oppressed that helped you when you complained of Oppression. Let not Pride blind your eyes, that you should forget you are the Nations Servants, and so prove *Solomons* words good in your selves, That Servants ride on Horse-back and Coaches, when as Princes, such as Chose you, and set you there, go on foot: and many of them, through their love to the Nation, have so wasted themselves, that now they can hardly get Bread, but with great difficulty. I tell you this is a sore Evil, and this is truth; therefore think upon it, it is a poor mans Advice, and you shall finde weight in it, if you Do as well as Say.

Then Secondly for Lords of Mannors, They were *William* the Conquerors Colonels and Favourites, and he gave a large circuit of Land to every one, called A Lord-ship, that they might have a watchful eye, that if any of the conquered English should begin to Plant themselves upon any Common or waste Land, to live out of sight or out of slavery, that then some Lord of Mannor or other might see and know of it, and drive them off, as these Lords of Mannors now a dayes, endeavours to drive off the Diggers from Digging upon the Commons; but we expect the Rulers of the Land will grant unto us their Friends, the benefit of their own Acts against Kingly power, and not suffer that Norman power to crush the poor Oppressed, who helped them in their straits, nor suffer that Norman power to bud fresher out, & so in time may come to over-top our deer bought Freedom more then ever.

Search all your Laws, and Ile adventure my life, for I have little else to lose, That all Lords of Mannors hold Title to the Commons by no stronger hold then the Kings Will, whose Head is cut off; and the King held Title as he was a Conqueror; now if you cast off the King who was the Head of that power, surely the power of Lords of Mannors is the same; therefore performe your own Act of Parliament, and cast out that part of the

Kinglie power likewise, that the People may see you understand what you Say and Do, and that you are faithful.

For truly the Kinglie power reigns strongly in the Lords of Mannors over the Poor; for my own particular, I have in other Writings as well as in this, Declared my Reasons, That the common Land is the poor Peoples Proprietie; and I have Digged upon the Commons, and I hope in time to obtain the Freedom, to get Food and Raiment therefrom by righteous labour, which is all I desire; and for so doing, the supposed Lord of that Mannor hath Arrested me twice; First, in an Action of 20.1. Trespass for Plowing upon the Commons, which I never did; and because they would not suffer me to Plead my own Cause, they made shift to pass a Sentence of Execution against some Cows I kept, supposing they had been mine, and took them away; but the right Owner reprieved them, & fetched the Cowes back; so greedy are these Theeves and Murderers after my life for speaking the truth, and for maintaining the Life and Marrow of the Parliaments Cause in my Actions.

And now they have Arrested me again in an Action of 4.1. trespas for digging upon the Comons, which I did, & own the work to be righteous & no trespas to any: This was the Attorney of *Kingstone*'s Advice, either to get Money on both sides, for they love Mony as deerly as a poor mans dog do his breakfast in a cold morning (but regard not justice) or else, That I should not remove it to a higher Court, but that the cause might be tryed there, and then they know how to please the Lords of Mannors, that have resolved to spend hundreds of pounds but they will hinder the poor from enjoying the Commons; for they will not suffer me to plead my own Cause, but I must not Fee an enemie, or else be condemned and executed without mercy or Justice as I was before, and so to put me in Prison till I pay their unrighteous Sentence; for truly Attorneys are such neat workmen, that they can turn a Cause which way those that have the biggest purse will have them: and the Countrie knows very well, That

Kingstone court is so full of the Kinglie power; that some will rather lose their Rights, then have their causes tryed there: one of the Officers of that court, told a friend of mine, That if the Diggers cause was good, he would pick out such a Jurie as should overthrow him: And upon my former Arrest, they picked out such a Jurie as Sentenced me to pay 10.1. damages for plowing upon the commons, which I did not do, neither did any witness prove it before them: So that from *Kingstone* Juries, Lords of Mannors, and Kinglie power, *Good Lord deliver us.*

Do these men obey the Parliaments Acts, to throw down Kinglie power? O no: The same unrighteous doing that was complained of in King *Charles* dayes, the same doings is among them still: Monies will buy and sell Justice still: and is our 8 yeers Wars come round about to lay us down again in the kennel of injustice as much or more then before? are we no farther learned yet? O ye Rulers of *England*, when must we turn over a new leaf? will you alwayes hold us in one Lesson? surely you will make Dunces of us; then all the Boyes in other Lands will laugh at us: come, I pray let us take forth, and go forward in our learning.

You blame us who are the Common people as though we would have no government; truly Gentlemen, We desire a righteous government with all our hearts, but the government we have gives freedom and livelihood to the Gentrie, to have abundance, and to lock up Treasures of the Earth from the poor, so that rich men may have chests full of Gold and Silver, and houses full of Corn and Goods to look upon; and the poor that works to get it, can hardly live, and if they cannot work like Slaves, then they must starve. And thus the Law gives all the Land to some part of mankind whose Predecessors got it by conquest, and denies it to others, who by the righteous Law of Creation may claim an equall portion; and yet you say this is a righteous government, but surely it is no other but self-ishness, which is the great Red Dragon, the Murtherer.

England is a Prison; the variety of subtilties in the Laws preserved by the Sword, are bolts, bars, and doors of the prison; the
Lawyers are the Jaylors, and poor men are the prisoners; for let
a man fall into the hands of any from the Bailiffe to the Judge,
and he is either undone, or wearie of his life.

Surely this power the Laws, which is the great Idoll that
people dote upon, is the burden of the Creation, a Nurserie
of Idleness, luxurie, and cheating, the only enemie of Christ
the King of righteousness; for though it pretend Justice, yet the
Judges and Law-Officers, buy and sell Justice for money, and
wipes their mouths like *Solomons* whore, and says it is my calling, and never are troubled at it.

Two things must cast out this Idoll: First, Let not people send
their children to those Nurseries of Covetousness, *The Innes of
Court*. Secondly, let not people live in contention, but fulfill
Christs last commandment, *Love*; and endeavour to practice that
full point of the Law and the Prophets, *Doe as you would be done
by*, and so cast out envie and discontent. Woe to you Lawyers,
for your trade is the bane and miserie of the world; your power
is the only power that hinders Christ from rising; the destruction of your power will be the life of the World; it is full of
confusion, it is Babylon, and surely its fall is neer, in regard the
light of truth is rising, who will continue your power, but save
your persons by the words of his mouth, and brightnesse of his
coming.

The Lawyers trade is one of the false Prophets, that says, Lo
here is Christ, Ile save you in this Court, and lo there is Christ,
Ile save you in that Court: but when we have tried all, we are
lost, and not saved, for we are either utterly made Beggars by
this Saviour, the Law, or else we are nursed up in hardnesse of
heart and cruelty against our fellow creature whom we ought
to love and preserve, and not destroy: This Saviour jeeres righteousness, and bids every man save himself, and never regard
what becomes of another, and so is a plain destroyer of the

Creation; Surely that Wo pronounced against Lawyers by the Man Christ must be fulfilled, delay is no payment: Therefore you Parliament and Army that have power in your hands, reform the Law; and suffer none to be called to practice Law but reformed ones; nay suffer every man to plead his own cause, and choose his own Lawyer, where he finds the most ingenuous man: Wel, every mans burthen in this Age fills their mouths with words of Lamentation against Law and Lawyers sufficiently; therefore you that have an opportunitie to ease the cry of the oppressed, shut not your eies and eares, but cast out this covetous corruption whereby corrupt Lawyers doe oppress the People; it is another Branch of the Kingly power.

You Gentlemen of *Surrey*, and Lords of Mannors, and you Mr Parson *Platt*[3] especially, that lay almost a fortnight waiting and tempting the Lord *Fairfax* to send Souldiers to drive off the Diggers, when he granted your Desire, it was but to secure the Shereiff, for he did not give them commission to beat us, which we thank him for; and we thank the Souldiers for their moderation, that they would not strike poor wormes, *Englands* and the creations faithful friends, though you would have moved them thereunto. My Advice to you Gentlemen is this, Hereafter to lie still and cherish the Diggers, for they love you, and would not have your finger ake if they could help it; and why should you be so bitter against them? O let them live by you; some of them have been Souldiers, and some countrie-men that were alwayes friends to the Parliaments cause, by whose hardship and meanes you enjoy the creatures about you in peace; and will you now destroy part of them that have preserved your lives? O do not do so; be not so besotted with the Kinglie power; hereafter let not the Attourneyes or Lawyers neatly councel your Money out of your purses, and stir you up to beat and abuse the Diggers, to make all rational men laugh at your folly, and condemn you for your bitterness: If you have yet so much Money, give it not away to destroy men, but give it to some poor or other to be a

Stock, and bid them go and Plant the common; this will be your honour, and your comfort; assure your selves you never must have true comfort tell you be friends with the poor; therefore come, come, love the Diggers, and make restitution of their Land you from them; for what would you do if you had not such labouring men to work for you?

And you great Officers of the Army and Parliament, love your common Souldiers, (I plead for Equity and Reason) and do not force them by long delay of Payment to sell you their deer bought Debenters[4] for a thing of naught, and then to go and buy our common Land, and crown Land, and other Land that is the spoil one of another, therewith: Remember you are Servants to the commons of *England*, and you were Volunteers in the Wars, and the common people have paid you for your pains so largely, that some of us have not left our selves hardly bread to eat; and therefore if there be a spoil to be gathered of crown Lands, Deans, Bishops, Forrests Lands and commons, that is to come to the poor commons freely; and you ought to be content with your wages, unless you will denie Christ and the Scriptures; and you ought not to go and buy one of another that which is common to all the Nation; for you ought neither to buy nor sell other mens Proprietie by the Law of creation; for Christ gives you no such Warrant. As soon as you have freed the Earth from one intanglement of Kinglie power, will you intangle it more, and worse by another degree of Kinglie power? I pray consider what you do, and do righteously: We that are the poor commons, that paid our Money, and gave you free Quarter, have as much Right in those crown Lands and Lands of the spoil as you; therefore we give no consent That you should buy and sell our crown Lands and waste Lands, for it is our purchased inheritance from under Oppression, it is our own, even the poor common peoples of *England*: It was taken from us, and hath been held from us by former conquests, whereof the Norman conquest was the last, which is cast out by yours and our joynt Assistance; therefore you cannot in Equity take it from us, nor we cannot in Equity take it from you, for it is our joynt purchased inheritance; we paid you your wages to help us to recover it, but not to take it to your selves, and turn us out, and buy and sell it among your selves; for this is a cheat of the Kinglie swordlie power which you hold up; and we profess to all the world, in so doing you denie God, Christ, and the Scriptures whom ye professed you own: for God, Christ, and Scriptures owne no such practice: Likewise we profess to all the Creation, That in so doing, you rob us of our Rights; & you kill us, by denying to give us our livelihood in our own inheritance freely, which is the crown Land and Comon Land and waste Lands, Bishops & Deans, which some of you begin to say you are not satisfied in your conscience to let us have; I, well spoke tender hearted Covetousness; if you do so you will uphold the Kinglie power, and so disobey both Acts of Parliament, and break your Oath, and you will live in the breach of those Two Commandements, *Thou shalt not kill: Thou shalt not steal*; by denying us the Earth which is our Livelyhood, and thereby killing us by a lingring death.

Well, the end of all my Speech is to point out the Kingly power, where I spie it out, and you see it remains strongly in the hands of Lords of Mannors, who have delt discourteously with some who are sincere in heart, though there have some come among the Diggers that have caused scandall, but we dis-own their wayes.[5]

The Lords of Mannors have sent to beat us, to pull down our houses, spoil our labours; yet we are patient, and never offered any violence to them again, this 40 weeks past, but wait upon God with love till their hearts thereby be softened; and all that we desire is, but to live quietly in the land of our nativity, by our righteous labour, upon the common Land which is our own, but as yet the Lords of the Mannor so formerly called, will not suffer us, but abuse us. Is not that part of the Kingly power? In that which follows I shall cleerly prove it is, for it appears so cleer that the understanding of a child does say, It is Tyranny, it is the Kingly power of darkness, therefore we expect that you will grant us the benefit of your Act of Parliament that we may say, Truly *England* is a Common-wealth, and a free people indeed.

Sire, Though your Tithing Priests and others tell you, That we Diggers do deny God, Christ, and the Scripture, to make us odious, and themselves better thought of; yet you will see in time when the King of Righteousness whom we serve does cleer our innocencie, That our actions and conversation is the very life of the Scripture, and holds forth the true power of God and Christ. For is not the end of all preaching, praying, and profession wrapped up in this action, (namely, *Love your enemies, and doe to all men, as you would they should do to you, for this is the very Law and the Prophets.* This is the New Commandement that Christ left behind him. Now if any seem to say this, and does not do this, but acts contrary, for my part I owne not their wayes, they are members that uphold the curse.

Bare talking of righteousnesse, and not acting, hath ruled, and yet does rule king of darkness in the creation; and it is the cause of all this immoderate confusion and ignorance that is in men.

But the actings of righteousnesse from the inward power of love, shall rule King of righteousnesse to the creation now in these later dayes, and cast the other Serpent and fiery Scorpion out; for this is Christ the restoring power: and as he rises up, so multitude of words without action (which is hypocrisie) is to die, his judgment hastens apace.

If any sort of people hold the earth to themselves by the dark Kingly power, and shut out others from that freedom, they deny God, Christ, and Scriptures, and they overthrow all their preaching, praying, and profession; for the Scriptures declare them to be Hypocrites, Scribes and Pharisees, *that say, and do not*; they have words, and no deeds: Like Parson *Platt* the Preacher at *Horsley* in *Surrey*, a Lord of Mannor (by marriage) of the place where we digg, who caused a poor old mans house that stood upon the Common, to be pulled down in the evening of a cold day, and turned the old man, and his wife, and daughter to lie in the open field, because he was a Digger: and he, and other Lords of Mannors, and Gentlemen sent their servants up and down the Town, to bid their Tenants and neighbours, neither to give the Diggers lodging nor victuals, on pain of their displeasure. Though this Parson *Platt* preach the Scriptures, yet I'll affirm, he denyes God, Christ, and Scriptures, and knowes nothing of them; for covetousness, pride, and envie hath blinded his eyes. A man knowes no more of righteousness than he hath power to act; and surely, this cruelty of preaching *Platt* is an unrighteous act.

If the Diggers were enemies, (oh you Lords of Mannors) as they are not, you ought to love them: I am sure, they love you; and if you doubt it, put them to the tryall; you shall find them more faithfull than many of those pick-thank slaves, and belly-god servants to whom your ears are open, when they bring tales full of envie to you against us.

We are told likewise, That to make us who are called Diggers, odious, and to incense you against us, there came to the Generall and Councell of State, divers Justices, and others, and told you, that we Diggers were Cavaliers, and that we waited an opportunity, and gathered together to stand up for the Prince.[6]

But all that know us can prove that to be a false report, to the dishonour of those Justices; for we have been friends to the Parliaments cause, and so do continue, and will continue; for this work of digging, to make *England* a free Commonwealth, is the life and marrow of the Parliaments cause. And the two Acts of Parliament, the One, to cast out Kingly power, the Other, to make *England* a free Common-wealth, declares it: and we do obey those Acts, and will obey them, for they hold forth righteousnesse.

But for our rising in arms for the Prince, or any other, let any come and see our strength and work, and they will say, It is a meer envious slander cast upon us, to incense you against us.

Besides, You shall see by and by, That our principles are wholly against Kingly power in every one, as well as in one. Likewise we hear, that they told you, that the Diggers do steal and rob from others. This likewise is a slander: we have things stollen from us; but if any can prove that any of us do steal any mans proper goods, as Sheep, Geese, Pigs, as they say, let such be made a spectacle to all the world: For my part, I own no such doing, neither do I know any such thing by any of the Diggers. Likewise they report, that we Diggers hold women to be common, and live in that bestialnesse: For my part, I declare against it; I own this to be a truth, That the earth ought to be a common Treasury to all; but as for women, *Let every man have his own wife, and every woman her own husband*; and I know none of the Diggers that act in such an unrationall excesse of female communitie: If any should, I professe to have nothing to do with such people, but leave them to their own Master, who will pay them with torment of minde, and diseases in their bodies.

These and such-like tales, we hear, are brought to you, to incense you against us: but we desire you to mark them that bring them, for we partly know who they be, and we can tell them to their faces, they were Cavaliers, and had hands in the Kentish Rising, and in stirring up that offensive *Surrey* Petition, which was the occasion of bloodshed in *Westminster*-yard,[7] and they would rejoyce to see the Prince come in with an Armie to over-top you: for we know, they love you not but from the teeth outwards, for their own ends: And these are the proud *Hamans*, that would incense you against the *Mordecaies* of the Land, even your true-hearted friends, the Diggers. Well, in the midst of our slanders we rejoyce in the uprightness of our hearts, and we do *commit our cause to him that judgeth righteously*.

Upon these lying reports, and importunitie to the General, it seems the General granted the Lords of Mannor to have some souldiers to go along with the Sheriff, to pull down the Diggers houses; and so the souldiers did come: but they were very moderate and rationall men, and as they were sent to secure the Sheriff, so they did: but there was no cause; for, though the Gentlemen possess'd the General, that they feared opposition from the Diggers, yet the souldiers saw they lifted not up a finger in discontent, but fought against those dragons, the Lords of Manors, with the spirit of love and patience: for when the two Lords of Manor sat among the souldiers on horsback and coach, and commanded their fearfull tenants to pull down one of the Diggers houses before their faces, and rejoyced with shouting at the fall; yet some of the Diggers stood by, and were very chearfull, and preached the Gospel to those Turkish *Bashaws*, which are words of life, and in time will prove words of terrour, to torment their awakened consciences.

And the poor tenants that pulled down the house, durst do no other, because their Land-lords and Lords looked on, for fear they should be turned out of service, or their livings; as a poor honest man, because he looked with a cheerfull countenance upon the Diggers (though he was affraid to come neer, or affraid to speak openly, lest his Landlords setting-dogs should smell the sound of his words, and carry a pick-thank tale, which his Lords ears are much open to) a Baily was sent presently to him, to warn him out of his house.

Can the Turkish Bashaws hold their slaves in more bondage than these Gospel-professing Lords of Manors do their poor tenants? and is not this the Kingly power? O you rulers of *England*, I pray see that your acts be obeyed, and let the oppressed go free.

And when the poor enforced slaves had pulled down the house, then their Lords gave them ten shillings to drink, and there they smiled one upon another; being fearfull, like a dog that is kept in awe, when his Master gives him a bone, and stands over him with a whip; he will eat, and look up, and twinch his tail; for they durst not laugh out, lest their Lords should hear they jeer'd them openly; for in their hearts they are Diggers. Therefore, you Lords of Manors, if you have none to stand for you but whom you force by threatning, then leave off striving against the spirit, and say you are fallen, and come in and embrace righteousnesse, that you may finde mercy betimes.

The next day after this, there came two souldiers and three Country-men to another house which the Diggers had set up, (which the Sheriff the day before had let alone, for, as some say, he was grieved to see what was done,) one of these souldiers was very civill, and walked lovingly with the Diggers round their corn which they had planted, and commended the work, and would do no harm (as divers others were of the same minde) and when he went his way, gave the Diggers 12d. to drink: but the other souldier was so rude, that he forced those three Country-men to help him to pull down the house, and railed bitterly: the men were unwilling to pull it down; but for fear of their Landlords, and the threatening souldier, they did put their hands to pull it down.

And seeing Parson *Platt* (the Lord of that Manor) will not suffer the Diggers to have a house, (wherein he forgets his Master Christ, that is persecuted in naked, hungry, and house-lesse members) yet the Diggers were mighty cheerfull, and their spirits resolve to wait upon God, to see what he will do, and they have built them some few little hutches like calf-cribs, and there they lie anights, and follow their work adayes still with wonderfull joy of heart, taking the spoyling of their goods cheerfully, counting it a great happinesse to be persecuted for righteousnesse sake, by the Priests and Professors, that are the successors of *Judas*, and the bitter-spirited Pharisees that put the man Christ *Jesus* to death. And they have planted divers Acres of Wheat and Rye, which is come up, and promises a very hope-full crop, committing their cause to God, and wait upon him, saying, O thou King of righteousnesse, do thine own work.

O that you would search and try our wayes narrowly, and see whether we deny God, Christ, Scriptures, as the Priests slander us we do; and you shall finde, that the Scriptures warrant our action, and God in Christ is the life of our souls, and the support of our spirits in the midst of this our sharp persecution from the hands of unreasonable men, who have not faith in Christ, but uphold the Kingly power, which you have Voted down.

Likewise, you shall see, that we live in the performance of that work which is the very life and marrow of the Parliaments Cause, whereby we honour the Parliament and their Cause: as you shall see by this following Declaration, unfolding the foundation whereupon *Englands* Laws are, or the Freedom of a Commonwealth ought to be built, which is Equity and Reason.

In the time of the Kings, who came in as Conquerors, and ruled by the power of the Sword, not only the Common land, but the Inclosures also were captivated under the will of those Kings, till now of late that our later Kings granted more freedom to the Gentry than they had presently after the Conquest; yet under bondage still: for what are prisons, whips and gallows in the times of peace, but the laws and power of the sword, forcing and compelling obedience, and so enslaving, as if the sword raged in the open field?

England was in such a slavery under the Kingly power, that both Gentry and Commonaltie groaned under bondage; and to ease themselves, they endeavoured to call a Parliament, that by their counsels and decrees they might find some freedom.

But *Charles* the then King perceiving that the Freedom they strove for, would derogate from his Prerogative-tyranny, therupon he goes into the North, to raise a War against the Parliament, and took WILLIAM *the conqueror's* Sword into his hand again, thereby to keep under the former conquered English, and to uphold his Kingly power of self-will and Prerogative, which was the power got by former Conquests; that is, to rule over the lives and estates of all men at his will, and so to make us pure slaves and vassals.

Well, This Parliament, that did consist of the chief Lords, Lords of Manors, and Gentry, and they seeing that the King, by raising an Army, did thereby declare his intent to enslave all sorts to him by the sword; and being in distresse, and in a low ebb, they call upon the common people to bring in their Plate, Moneys, Taxes, Free-quarter, Excise, and to adventure their lives with them, and they would endeavour to recover *England* from that *Norman* yoak, and make us a free people: and the common people assent hereunto, and call this the Parliaments Cause, and own it, and adventure person and purse to preserve it; and by the joynt assistance of Parliament and People, the King was beaten in the field, his head taken off, and his Kingly power voted down; and we the Commons thereby virtually have recovered our selves from the Norman Conquest, we want nothing but possession of the spoyl, which is a free use of the Land for our livelyhood.

And from hence we the common people, or younger brothers, plead our propriety in the Common land, as truly our own by vertue of this victory over the King; as our elder brothers can plead proprietie in their Inclosures; and that for three reasons in *Englands* law.

First, By a lawfull purchase or contract between Parliament and us; for they were our Landlords and Lords of Mannors that held the freedom of the Commons from us, while the King was in his power; for they held title thereunto from him, he being the head, and they branches of the Kingly power, that enslaved the people by that ancient Conquerors Sword, that was the ruling power: For they said, Come and help us against the King that enslaves us, that we may be delivered from his Tyranny, and we will make you a free People.

Now they cannot make us free, unlesse they deliver us from the bondage which they themselves held us under; and that is, they held the freedom of the Earth from us: for we in part with them have delivered our selves from the King: now we claim freedom from that bondage you have, and yet do hold us under, by the bargain and contract between Parliament and us, who (I say) did consist of Lords of Manors, and Landlords, whereof Mr. *Drake*, who hath arrested me for digging upon the Common, was one at that time: Therefore by the law of Bargain and Sale, we claim of them our freedom, to live comfortably with them in this Land of our Nativity; and this we cannot do, so long as we lie under poverty, and must not be suffered to plant the commons and waste land for our livelihood: for, take away the land from any people, and those people are in a way of continu-all death and misery; and better not to have had a body, than not to have food and rayment for it. But (I say) they have sold us our freedom in the common, and have been largely paid for it; for by means of our bloods and money, they sit in peace: for if the King had prevailed, they had lost all, and been in slavery to the meanest Cavalier, if the King would. Therefore we the Commons say, Give us our bargain: if you deny us our bargain, you deny God, Christ, and Scriptures; and all your profession then is and hath been hypocrisie.

Secondly, The Commons and Crown land is our propriety by equall conquest over the Kingly power: for the Parl. did never stir up the people by promises and covenant to assist them to cast out the King, and to establish them in the Kings place and prerogative power: No, but all their Declarations were for the safety and peace of the whole Nation.

Therefore the common-people being part of the Nation, and especially they that bore the greatest heat of the day in casting out the oppressor: and the Nation cannot be in peace, so long as the poor oppressed are in wants, and the land is intangled and held from them by bondage.

But the Victory being obtained over the King, the spoyl which is properly the Land, ought in equity to be divided now between the two Parties, that is, Parliament and Common-people. The Parliament, consisting of Lords of Manors, and Gentry, ought to have their inclosure Lands free to them without molestation, as they are freed from the Court of Wards.[8]

And the Common-people, consisting of Souldiers, and such as paid Taxes and Free-quarter, ought to have the freedom of all waste and common land, and Crown-land equally among them; the Souldiery ought not in equity to have all, nor the other people that paid them to have all; but the spoyle ought to be divided between them that stay'd at home, and them that went to Warr; for the Victory is for the whole Nation.

And as the Parliament declared, they did all for the Nation, and not for themselves onely; so we plead with the Armie, they did not fight for themselves, but for the freedom of the Nation: and I say, we have bought our Freedom of them likewise by Taxes and Free-quarter: therefore we claim an equall Freedom with them in this Conquest over the King.

Thirdly, We claim an equall portion in the Victory over the King, by vertue of the two Acts of Parliament, the One to make *England* a Free-Common-wealth; the Other to take away Kingly power. Now the Kingly power (you have heard) is a power that rules by the Sword in covetousnesse and self, giving the earth to some, and denying it to others: and this Kingly power was not in the hand of the King alone; but Lords, and Lords of Manors, and corrupt Judges, and Lawyers especially, held it up likewise; for he was the head, and they, with the Tything-priests are the branches of that Tyrannical Kingly power; and all the several limbs and members must be cast out, before Kingly power can be pulled up root and branch. Mistake me not, I do not say, Cast out the persons of men: No, I do not desire their fingers to ake: but I say, Cast out their power, whereby they hold the people in bondage, as the King held them in bondage. And I say, it is our own Freedom we claim, both by bargain, and by equality in the Conquest; as well as by the Law of righteous Creation, which gives the Earth to all equally.

And the power of Lords of Mannors lies in this: They deny the Common people the use and free benefit of the Earth, unless they give them leave, and pay them for it, either in Rent, in Fines, in Homages, or Heriots. Surely the Earth was never made by God, that the Younger brother should not live in the Earth, unless he would work for, and pay his Elder brother Rent for the Earth: No; this Slavery came in by Conquest, and it is part of the Kingly power; and *England* cannot be a Free Common-wealth, till this Bondage be taken away. You have taken away the King; you have taken away the House of Lords:[9] Now step two steps further, and take away the power of Lords of Mannors, and of Tything Priests, and the intolerable oppressions of Judges, by whom Laws are corrupted; and your work will be honourable.

Fourthly, if this Freedom be denied the Common people, To enjoy the Common Land; then Parliament, Army and Judges will deny Equity and Reason, whereupon the Laws of a well-governed Common-wealth ought to be built: And if this Equity be denied then there can be no Law, but Club-Law, among the people: and if the Sword must raign, then every Party will be striving to bear the Sword; and then farewel Peace; nay, farewel Religion and Gospel, unless it be made use of to intrap one another, as we plainly see some Priests and others make it a Cloke for their Knavery. If I adventure my life, and fruit of my labour, equal with you, and obtain what we strive for; it is both Equity and Reason, that I should equally divide the Spoil with you, and not you to have all, and I none: And if you deny us this, you take away our Propriety from us, our Moneys and Blood, and give us nothing for it.

Therefore, I say, the Common Land is my own Land, equal with my fellow-Commoners; and our true Propriety, by the Law of Creation: it is every ones, but not one single ones: Yea, the Commons are as truely ours by the last excellent two Acts of Parliament, the Foundation of *Englands* new righteous Government aimed at, as the Elder brothers can say the Inclosures are theirs: for they adventured their Lives, and covenanted with us to help them to preserve their Freedom: And we adventured our lives, and they covenanted with us, to purchase and to give us our Freedom, that hath been hundreds of yeers kept from us.

Daemona non Armis, sed Morte subegit Iesus.[10]

> *By patient Sufferings, not by Death,*
> *Christ did the Devil kill;*
> *And by the same, still to this day,*
> *his Foes he conquers still.*

True Religion, and undefiled, is this, To make restitution of the Earth, which hath been taken and held from the Common people, by the power of Conquests formerly, and so *set the oppressed free*. Do not All strive to enjoy the Land? The Gentry strive for Land, the Clergie strive for Land, the Common people strive for Land; and Buying and Selling is an Art, whereby people endeavour to cheat one another of the Land. Now if any can prove, from the Law of Righteousness, that the Land was made peculiar to him and his successively, shutting others out, he shall enjoy it freely, for my part: But I affirm, It was made for all; and true Religion is, To let every one enjoy it. Therefore, you Rulers of *England*, make restitution of the Lands which the Kingly power holds from us: *Set the oppressed free*; and come in, and honour Christ, who is the Restoring Power, and you shall finde rest.

THE *CURSE* AND *BLESSING* THAT IS IN *MANKINDE.*

In the beginning of Time, the Spirit of Universal Love appeared to be the father of all things: The Creation of Fire, Water, Earth, and Air, came out of him, and is his clothing. *Love* is the *Word.*

The Creation is the House or Garden, in which this one Spirit hath taken up his seat, and in which he manifests himself: For if ever Love be seen or known, he appears either in the inward feeling within your hearts, loving All with tender love; or else appears towards you, from outward objects, as from other Men, or other creatures.

There are two Earths, in which the Spirit of Love declares himself. First, the Living Earth, called *Mankinde*: this is the Creation, or the living soul. And when this Spirit of universal Love rules King therein, this Earth is then in peace, and is grown up to the perfection of a man anointed. But when Self or Particular love rules, which is called the sin Covetousness, then this Earth is brought into Bondage, and Sorrow fills all places. This is the dark side of the Cloud, in which there is no true peace.

Secondly, in the great Body of Earth in which all creatures subsist, the Spirit of Universal Love appears, to preserve his Creation in peace: for Universal Love unites not onely Mankinde into an oneness, but unites all other creatures into a sweet harmony of willingness to preserve Mankinde. And this Spirit of Love spread abroad, is the same Spirit of Love that is supreme in Man: and this is the Righteous man.

But when Covetousness or Particular love began to work, then not onely Mankinde was divided amongst themselves, but all creatures were divided, and enmity rose up amongst them, setting one against another; and this power is the wicked man: mark him where you see him, which is the Murderer, and must be cast out.

Wel, In the begining, universal love appeared to be the father of al things, (though self-love in our experience rules in man first) and as he made mankinde to be the Lord of the Earth, so he made the Earth to be a common Treasury of livelihood to whole mankind without respect of persons; and for all other creatures likewise that were to proceed from the Earth.

Mankind is the chief creature, and the Spirit of universal Love in his branches, is the Lord of all the Earth; and this Spirit in man unfolds himself in Light and Darkness: his face is called the universal power of Love: his back parts is called the selvish power: or thus, the one is called the Son of Bondage which causes shame, the other is called the Son of Freedom, which brings peace and honour: these Two strive in the womb of the Earth which shal come forth first; and which shall rule; the fleshly man, hath got the start; but the other will prove the stronger, and cast him out with honour.

While this Spirit of Lordship in the last day time of mankind, was universal Love and Righteousness leading every single branch of mankind to do to another as he would be done unto; then every thing was in peace, and there was a sweet communion of Love in the creation: and as the Spirit was a common Treasurie of Unitie and Peace within, so the Earth was a common Treasurie of delight for the preservation of their bodies without, so that there was nothing but peace upon the face of the whole Earth.

This was mans estate, before the fall or the day time of mankind; for since the time that our Bibles speak of *Adam* to this day, is about 6000 yeers; and this time hath been the night time of mankind: and *Esays* time was about midnight when in one of his words he cries, *Watchman, What of the night? Watchman, What of the night?* the seventh thousand yeer which is now dawning, will be the rising of the Son of universal Love again, and of the dispersing of the night or darkness; for as the night and day Sun and Moon hath their exchanges, so hath these Two powers, called Sons of God in mankind; and in this age wherein we now live is the expiring of the selvish power, and the rising up of the

Blessing which hath been spoke of in al ages, but now appearing like lightning from east to west, casting out the Mysterie of Iniquitie, or self power, by the word of his mouth, and by the brightness of his comming, and so bringing peace.

So that, as there is the power of Light, which is universal Love, called the Blessing which brings Peace; so there is the power of Darkness, which is particular or self love, and this is called the Curse, for it brings sorrow: and while this rules King in the Earth, as it doth at this day visibly through the whole Earth, few are saved, that is, few enter into rest and peace; for this power hath filled all places, with his stinking self seeking Government, and troubles every body.

As there is light and darkness, day and night, clouds and cleerness moving upon the face of the great Earth; and as there is Earth and Waters in the great World which runs round; so mankind is called sometimes Earth, some times Waters; and as the Sun in the skies moves upon the great Earth and makes that fruitful which seemed dead, while the Sun is under the dark cloudy winter quarter:

Even so the Son of universal Love, who is the Spirit and power of universal Freedom, he moves upon the living waters mankind, and makes him, who all the dark time past was a Chaos of confusion, lying under Types, Shadows, Ceremonies, Forms, Customes, Ordinances, and heaps of waste words, under which the Spirit of Truth lay buried, now to enlighten, to worship in Spirit and Truth, and to bring forth fruit of Righteousness in action.

In our present experience, The darkness or self-love goeth before; and light or universal love follows after; the flesh runs hasty and quick, and loses himself in unrational excessive action; the true Spirit comes slowly after, and takes the Crown.

Darkness and Bondage, doth oppress Liberty and Light; and the power of universal Love appears most sweet and full of glory, when the power of self Love or Covetousness hath tortured the

Creation (mankind) with bitter Tyranny: for this is the Dragon or Murderer that must be cast out; before the Creation (man) can sing *Halelujah* in peace.

So then you may see, That the innocency, light, and purity of mankind is this, when the Spirit of universal Love lives in him, and he lives in Love, enjoying the sweet Union and communion of Spirit, each with other.

When they enjoy the sweet delight of the Unitie of one Spirit, and the free content of the fruits and crops of this outward Earth, upon which their bodies stand: this was called The mans innocency, or pleasure in the Garden before his fall, or the day time of mankind; and day is more glorious then night; and greater honour to be a child of the day, then of the night.

The fall of mankind, or his darkness is this, When that Son of universal Love, which was the seed, out of which the creation sprung forth, did begin to go behind the cloud of flesh, and to let self-seeking flesh which would needs be a God, stand alone by his imaginary light, as we see, while the Sun is in the skies, a man sees and knows his footsteps, but when the Sun is set under the cloud of the dark night, then he imagins his way, and oft times stumbles and falls:

Even so, when universal Love shines in his glory in mankind, he stumbles not, he walks in the light, because the light is in him; but when the light within with drawes and lets flesh stand alone, Flesh, that is, The selvish power will not wait in peace, and acknowledge himself in a loss and in darkness, till the Sun rise again:

But will fain be a God, and calls his weakness strength; and though there appears nothing but deformity, yet he would have it called beauty; and because his inward power is not sutable to his outward profession, he is tormented: he is a Saint without, but a Devil within: but if thou wouldest have peace, act as thou art, shew thy self abroad in action what thou art secretly; but when thou beginst to imagine a content and happiness to thy self, by thy hypocritical self invention, then thou art tormented, or shalt be.

And by this imagination, mankind tears himself in pieces; as one of your Colonels of the Army said to me, *That the Diggers did work upon* George Hill *for no other end but to draw a company of People into Arms*; and sayes *our knavery is found out, because it takes not that effect.*

Truly thou Colonel, I tell thee, Thy knavish imagination is thereby discovered, which hinders the effecting of that Freedom which by Oath and Covenant thou hast Engaged to maintain: for my part, and the rest, we had no such thought; we abhor fighting for Freedom, it is acting of the Curse and lifting him up higher; and do thou uphold it by the Sword, we will not; we will conquer by Love and Patience, or else we count it no Freedom: Freedom gotten by the Sword is an established Bondage to some part or other of the Creation; and this we have Declared publickly enough; therefore thy imagination told thee a lye, and will deceive thee in a greater matter, if Love doth not kill him: Victory that is gotten by the Sword, is a Victory that slaves gets one over another; and hereby *men of the basest Spirit* (saith *Daniel*) *are set to Rule:* but Victory obtained by Love, is a Victory for a King.

But by this you may see what a liar imagination is, and how he makes bate, and tears the Creation in pieces; for after that self Love hath subdued others under him, then imagination studies how to keep himself up and keep others down.

This is your very inward Principle, O ye present powers of *England*, you do not study how to advance universal Love; if you did, it would appear in action: but imagination and self-love mightily disquiets your mind, and makes you call up all the powers of darknesse to come forth and help to set the Crown upon the head of Self, which is that Kinglie power you have Oathed and Vowed against, and yet uphold it in your hands.

Imagination begets Covetousnesse after pleasure, honour, and riches: Covetousnesse begets Fear, least others should crosse them in their Design; or else begets a Fear of want, and this makes a man to draw the creatures to him by hook or crook, and to please the strongest side, looking what others do, not minding what himself doth.

Like some of your great Officers, that told me, *That we Diggers took away other mens Propriety from them, by Digging upon the Common*; yet they have taken mine and other mens proprietie of money (got by honest labour) in Taxes and free-quarter to advance themselves and not allow us that they promised us; for it this beam in their own eies they cannot see.

This Fear begets hypocrisie, subtlety, envie, and hardness of heart, which makes a man to break all promises and engagements, and to seek to save himself in others ruine, and to suppresse and oppresse every one that does not say as he sayes, and do as he does.

And this hardness of heart begets pride and security, and this begets luxurie and lust of the flesh, and this runs into all excesse with greedines, and being in discontent against any that crosses his pleasure, till his heart become fully like the heart of a Beast, as it is apparent in some at this day.

And thus by the power of self-love being advanced by the covetous sword against universall love, that power of darkness rises up to perfection in mankind, and so he makes one branch to tear and devour another by divisions, evill surmisings, envious fightings, and killing, and by oppressing the meek in Spirit, by unrighteous Laws, or by his self will managing good laws unrighteously, as corrupt Judges know how to do it, and think none sees them, whereby part of mankind hath freedom, and another part is cast out and thrown under bondage.

And all this falling out or quarrelling among mankind, is about the earth who shall, and who shall not enjoy it, when indeed it is the portion of every one, and ought not to be striven for, nor bought, nor sold, whereby some are hedged in, and others hedged out; for better not to have had a body, then to be debarred the fruit of the Earth to feed and cloth it; and if every one did but quietly enjoy the earth for food and raiment, there would be no wars, prisons, nor gallows, and this action which man calls theft would be no sin, for universall love never made it a sin, but the power of covetousness made that a sin, and made Laws to punish it, though he himself live in that sin in a higher manner, then he hangs or punisheth. Those very men that punish others for theft do theeve and rob, as Judges and Lawyers that take Bribes, or that takes their Clients money, and through neglect lose their cause: Parliament and Army lives in Theft, when as they take the Commoners money, and free-quarter, and tell them what they do is to make *England* a free Common-Wealth, and yet all they doe is to make the Gentry free, and leaves the Commoners under bondage still; or else why do you send your Souldiers to beat a few naked Spademen off from digging the Commons for a livelihood, why do you not let the oppressed go free? have they not bought it of you by their monies and blood as well as the Gentrie, and will not you make good your Contract: Well, he that made the earth for us as well as for you will set us free though you will not: when will the Vail of darknes be drawn off your faces? will you not be wise O yee Rulers?

Well, this power of darknes is mans fall, or the right time of mankind.

But Universall love hath declared that he will rise again, and he himself who is the Seed, will bruise that Serpents head, and reconcile mankind to himself again, and restore him to that Innocencie and Peace which he is fallen from. When this Son arises in more strength, and appears to be the Saviour indeed, he will then make mankind to be all of one heart and one mind, and make the Earth to be a common treasurie, though for the present in outward view there is nothing but darkness and confusion upon the face of the earth, mankind.

When self love began to arise in the earth, then man began to fall, this is *Adam* or the power of darkness that stops up the waters and wel springs of life, or the clouds that hide the Son of righteousness from man.

This *Adam* or dark power was small at the first, but he is risen to great strength, and the whole Earth is now filled with him, as *Isiah* saith, *Darknes hath covered the Earth*, mankind. For let any that hath eyes look either to them above or them below, and they see darknes or the Devil rule, and this curse destroys the Earth. The Creation sits like *Rachel* sighing, mourning, and groaning under his oppressing power, and will not be comforted because they see no saviour to appear for their deliverance.

Indeed there are many saviours in word, but none in deed, and these great false Christs and false Prophets, does destroy the Creation under the colour of saving it, and the people sees them not, but looks upon them as saviours, calling others false Christs and false Prophets that speak against them.

The first false christ that promises to save the Creation, is covetous Kingly power, resting in the hand of one man, or in the hand of many, but this power saves but part, and holds another part of the creation in bondage, and any government that rules by swordly power doth so throughout all lands; therefore he is a false Christ, and no true saviour.

The Preaching Clergie or universative power, promises to save the Creation declaratively, but he is a false Christ, he saith and doth not, Pharisee-like, but will force people to maintain him from the Earth by their labours, for his sayings, by the Laws of the Kingly power; he saith, some are elected to salvation, and others are reprobated; he puts some into heaven, thrusts others into hell never to come out, and so he is not a universall Saviour; that is no salvation to the creation, mankind, while any part groans for the true Saviour, when he comes he will wipe away all teares, he comes not to destroy any but to save all.

Then the power of the Lawyers, he saith he will save the Creation, and this false Christ proves the greatest devourer and tearer of the creation of any other, for while he carries burthened men from one court to another promising to save them, he at last saves himself and destroyes others, and laughs at others losse, and throwes men further from peace then he found them before he medled with them: Well, From the Bailiffe to the Judge, these are the creations of this Egyptian Taskmaster, and no burthen of cheating like to it, for he promises Justice, but behold nothing but oppression is in his hands.

Then next, The Art of buying and selling promises to save the Creation, and bring it into peace, but this is a hypocriticall false cheating christ too, for hereby covetous self-love with his flattering tongue cheats honest hearted ones, and casts them under tyranny, and gets the fulness of the Earth into his hands, and lock it up in chests and barns from others, and saith this is righteous, and God gave it him, but thou cheater, thou liest; God the King of righteousness gave it thee not, he bids thee sell all that thou hast and give to the poor, he doth not bid thee lock it up from the poor, therefore thou trading art, thou art no true saviour neither, but a Devil, thou savest part, and destroyest another part, yea and afterwards destroyest that part which at first thou seemedst to save.

Now all these saviours are linked together, if one truly fall all must fall, they all promise to save the Creation, but destruction is in their hands and actions, they all seek to set up self and particular power, and so to save but part of the creation, for every one are destroyers of universall love: They that sit in these seats would be called men of publike Spirits, but truly you are all selfish, you are afraid to own publike spirited men, nay you are ashamed some of you to be seen walking or talking with true publike spirited men, called *Levellers*.

But well, yet there is a promise of restoration and salvation to the whole creation, and this must be wrought by a power contrary to darkness, for all those former saviours lie under darkness, nay are branches of the power of darkness it self, and darkness can never kill darkness; but now the true Saviour must be a power quite opposite to darkness: And this is,

The power of Universall Love, light and righteousness and if ever the creation be wholly saved, this power must be the saviour, for this is the blessing, and he will declare himself the true Saviour indeed, the other is but the curse, this is the true restorer, the true seed with us, as he arises and spreads, he will bruise the Serpents head in every one, and bring peace to all, and wipe away all tears from the creation, and make a through salvation of it through the whole earth, and leave none under bondage.

This is the Sun of righteousness when he ariseth, he disperseth darkness, and will make all ashamed that had hands in promoting of the other false saviours power; but I must leave this, and speak a little more of the present condition mankind lies under, and this is darknes or the fall, and in this estate ignorant inslaved flesh would ever run round in it, and never come out, but counts it freedom, but they that know the burthen of this estate hunger after freedom.

This darkness is twofold, first inward, and that is the power of darkness in his branchs, as covetousness, envy, pride, hypocrisie, self-love, this is the curse in man, and this darkness hath and yet doth cover the earth; this power would be as God, and makes one to rule over another, and he is so proud that he will hasten to rule though he kill others for honour, and this is he that stirs up wars and dissention, and thereby he destroyes himself.

Secondly this inward power sets one against another, and so fills the earth with dark actions, and causeth some part of mankind to tread others under foot and puts them into bondage, and they that act this power calls it, The power and Ordinance of God, which is true: It is God indeed, but it is the god of the world, the prince of darknes, not the King of Righteousnesse;

it is the power of the Beast who is limited to rule for a time, times, and dividing of time, and *England* is under that dividing of time, therefore I hope, *England* shall be the tenth part of the Citie confusion that shall fall from the Beast first:

And this dark power or imaginarie covetousnesse hath raised a platform of oppression in the creation, under which the creation groans, and waits to be delivered; and it is raised thus,

First this dark power within makes every one to love himself with others loss, just like Beasts of the Field; and this made mankind to begin to loath or envie each others Freedom and peace, and hereby the Union and Communion of Love within is broke and mankind is faln from it: then this inward Covetousnesse makes mankind to fight one against another for the Earth, and breaks Communion in that, and falls from content therein likewise, and every one seeks to save himself to take the Earth to himself, but none or few seeks the things of Christ, or of universal Love.

Nay Covetousnesse is such a god, that where he Rules he would have all the Earth to himself, and he would have all to be his servants, and his heart swels most against Communitie; calling Communitie a thief, that takes other mens Rights and Proprietie from them, but communitie will force nothing from any one, but take what is given in love, of that which others have wrought for; but no man yet hath bestowed any labour upon the Commons that lies waste; therefore the Diggers doth take no mans proper goods from them is so doing, but those that by force spoyls their labours, takes their proper goods from them, which is the fruit of their own labours.

Well, you see how Covetousnesse would have all the Earth to himself, though he let it lie waste: he stirs up Divisions among men, and makes parties fight against parties; and all is but for this, Who shall enjoy the Earth, and live in honour and ease and rule over others: and the stronger party alwayes rules over the weaker party.

And hence came in Kingly power to rule outwardly, dividing between members of that one body mankind, giving the Earth to that party called Gentry, who are the Successors of some late Conquests, and denying the Earth to the poor Commoners who are the Successors of some that were last Conquered.

So that by Kingly power the Earth is divided as it is now at this day: but as the Scriptures say, *Kings were given for a plague to the people, not a blessing:* And I beleeve the Nations have found this very true to their great sorrow: and the way to cast out Kingly power again, is not to cast them out by the Sword, for this doth but set him in more power, and removes him from a weaker to a stronger hand: but the only way to cast him out, is, For the People to leave him to himself, to forsake fighting and all oppression, and to live in love one towards another: This power of Love is, the true Saviour.

The party that is called a King, was but the head of an Army, and he and his Army having Conquered, shuts the conquered out of the Earth, and will not suffer them to enjoy it, but as a servant and slave to him; and by this power the creation is divided, and part are cast into bondage; so that the best you can say of Kingly power that Rules by the Sword is this, He is a murderer and a theif.

And by this power the Earth is thus divided.

The several Nations of the Earth where Kings rule, are the several situation of such grand Theeves and Murderers, that will rule over others by the Sword, upholding a forced Propriety, which is the Curse; and persecuting the community of Love, which is Christ the blessing.

And under them they have their cheif Favourits or neerest Souldiers in Office to himself, and to these he allows the greatest portion of the Earth, every one his part, called a Lordship: and next to them the inferior Officers or Souldiers, are appointed out lesser parcels of the Earth, called free-Holders, paying no slavish Rent or Homage to any: but only acknowledgment, That the King is their General or Head still.

And these Lords of Mannors and Free holders having thus seated themselves in the Earth, by taking other mens proper labours from them by the Sword, are appointed by the King as Watchmen. That if any of the conquered slaves seek to Plant the Common waste Earth without their leave, they may be known and beaten off: So that the god from whom they claim Title to the Land as proper to them, shutting out others, was Covetousnesse the Murderer, the swordly power, that great red Dragon, who is called, The god of the World.

But the King of Righteousnesse, who is universal Love, who is the Lord God Almighty, bidding every one *do as they would be done by*; made the Earth for All, without respect of person, and shuts out none from enjoying a peaceable livelihood that hath a body; therefore they that build upon the power of the Sword, upholding covetous Propriety, are enemies to the law of Righteousnesse, which is, *Love your enemies, do as you would be done by*.

But one of your Officers told me, *What?* (saith he) *If we grant to every one to have the Land of England in Common, we do not only destroy Propriety, but we do that which is not practised in any Nation in the world.*

I Answered, It was true; Propriety came in you see by the Sword, therefore the Curse; for the murderer brought it in, and upholds him by his power, and it makes a division in the Creation, casting many under bondage; therefore it is not the blessing, or the promised seed.

And what other Lands do, *England* is not to take pattern; for *England* (as well as other Lands) hath lyen under the power of that Beast, Kingly propriety: But now *England* is the first of Nations that is upon the point of Reforming: and if *England* must be the tenth part of the City *Babylon* that fals off from the Beast first, and would have that honour, he must cheerfully (and dally no longer) cast out Kingly covetous Propriety, and set the Crown upon Christs head, who is the universal Love or Free community, and so be the leader of that happy Restoration to all the Nations of the world: And if *England* refuse, some other Nation may be chosen before him, and *England* then shall lose his Crown, for if ever the Creation be Restored, this is the way which lies in this Two fold power:

First *Community of Mankind*, which is comprised in the unity of spirit of Love, which is called Christ in you, or the Law written in the heart, leading mankind into all truth, and to be of one heart and one mind.

The Second is *Community of the Earth*, for the quiet livelihood in food and raiment without using force, or restraining one another: These two Communities, or rather one in two branches, is that true Levelling, which Christ will work at his more glorious appearance; for Jesus Christ the Saviour of all men, is the greatest, first, and truest Leveller thet ever was spoke of in the world.

Therefore you Rulers of *England*, be not ashamed nor afraid of Levellers, hate them not, Christ comes to you riding upon these clouds; look not upon other Lands to be your pattern, all Lands in the world lie under darkness, so doth *England* yet, though the neerest to Light and Freedom of any other; therefore let no other Land take your Crown.

You have set Christ upon his throne in *England* by your Promises, Engagements, Oathes, and Two Acts of Parliament, the One to cast out Kingly power; the Other to make *England* a Free Commonwealth: Put all these into sincere Action, and you shall see the work is done, and you with others shall sing *Halelujah* to him that sits upon the Throne, and to the Lamb for evermore.

But if you do not, the Lamb shall shew himself a Lion, and tear you in pieces for your most abominable dissembling Hypocrisie, and give your Land to a People who better deserves it: I have varied a little, therefore I will return to what I was speaking.

I told you, *That the Murdering and Theeving Sword hath found out a Platform of Tyrannical Government, called Kingly Power.*

First here is the King, the Head of the murdering power, or great red Dragon.

Then there are Lords of Mannors, who have the greatest circuit of Land, because the next in Power to the Head.

Then there are Free-holders, that took the particular Inclosures which they found in a Land when they Conquered it, and had turned out those that had bestowed labour upon it, by force of the Sword, in the field, or else by sequestring afterwards: These several parcels of Land are called Free-hold-Land, because the Enjoyers or their Ancestors were Souldiers, and helped the King to conquer; and if any of latter yeers came to buy these Free-holds with Money got by Trading, it doth not alter the Title of the Conquest; for Evidences are made in the Kings Name, to remove the Free-holds so bought from one mans hand to another.

But now Copy-hold lands are parcels hedged in, and taken out of the common waste land since the conquest, acknowledging Homage, Fines, and Heriots to the Lord of that Mannor or circuit in which that Inclosure by his leave is made: this Homage still confirmes the power of the conquests.

The Lords of Mannors acknowledged Homage to the King in that Court of Wards, which you have taken away to ease your selves.

But the Copy-holders you will have to acknowledge Homage to Lords of Mannors still; and is not this partiality? O you Rulers, make the poor as free to the Earth as your selves, and honour Righteousnesse.[11]

Now for the drawing in of the People to yeeld Obedience to this Platform of Kingly tyrannical power, to which People are made subject through fear,

The Kingly power sets up a Preaching Clergy to draw the People by insinuating words to conform hereunto, and for their

pains Kingly power gives them the Tithes: And when the Kingly
power hath any Design to lift up himself higher, then the Clergy
is to Preach up that Design, as of late in our Wars the Preachers
most commonly in their Sermons medled with little but State
matters: and then if People seeme to deny Tythes, then the
Kingly power by his Lawes doth force the people to pay them:
so that there is a confederacie between the Clergy and the great
red Dragon: the Sheep of Christ shall never fare well so long as
the wolf or red Dragon payes the Shepherd their wages.

Then next after this, the Kingly power sets up a Law and
Rule of Government to walk by: and here Justice is preceded,
but the full strength of the Law is to uphold the conquering
Sword, and to preserve his son Propriety: therefore if any one
steal, this Law will hang them, and this they say is of God; and
so this Kingly power hath power over the lives and labours of
men at his pleasure; for though they say the Law doth punish,
yet indeed, that Law is but the strength, life and marrow of the
Kingly power, upholding the conquest still, hedging some into
the Earth, hedging out others; giving the Earth to some, and
denying the Earth to others, which is contrary to the Law of
Righteousnesse, who made the Earth at first as free for one as
for another.

Yea that Kingly power in the Lawes appointed the conquered
poor to work for them that possesse the Land, for three pence
and four pence a day, and if any refused, they were to be imprisoned; and if any walked a begging and had no dwelling, he was
to be whipt; and all was to force the slaves to work for them
that had taken their Propriety of their labours from them by the
Sword, as the Laws of *England* are yet extant, and truly most
Lawes are but to enslave the Poor to the Rich, and so they
uphold the conquest, and are Lawes of the great red Dragon.

And at this very day poor people are forced to work in some
places for 4, 5, and 6 pence a day; in other places for 8, 10, and
12 pence a day, for such small prizes now Corn being deer, that

their earnings cannot find them bread for their Family; and yet if they steal for maintenance, the murdering Law will hang them; when as Lawyers, Judges, and Court Officers can take Bribes by whole sale to remove one mans Propriety by that Law into another mans hands: and is not this worse theevery then the poor mans that steals for want? Well, this shewes, that if this be Law, it is not the Law of Righteousnesse; it is a Murderer, it is the Law of Covetousnesse and self-love; and this Law that frights people and forces people to obey it by Prisons, Whips, and Gallows, is the very kingdom of the Devil, and Darknesse, which the Creation groans under at this day.

And if any poor enslaved man that dares not steal, begins to mourn under that bondage and saith, We that work most have least comfort in the earth, and they that work not at all, enjoy all; contrary to the Scripture which saith, *The poor and the meek shall inherit the earth.*

Presently the tithing Priest stop his mouth with a slam and tels him that is meant of the inward satisfaction of mind which the poor shall have, though they enjoy nothing at all, and so poor creatures, it is true, they have some ease thereby, and made to wait with patience, while the Kingly power swims in fulness, and laughs at the others miserie; as a poor Cavalier Gentlewoman presented a Paper to the Generall in my sight, who looked upon the woman with a tender countenance; but a brisk little man and two or three more Colonels puld back the Paper not suffering the Generall to receive it, and laught at the woman who answered them again, I thought said she, you had not sate in the seat of the scornfull; this was done in *Whitehall* upon the 12. of *December* 1649.[12]

Well, all that I shall say to these men that will enjoy the earth in realitie, and tell others they must enjoy it in conceit, surely your judgement from the most High sleepeth not; the Law of Retaliation like for like, laughing for laughing may be your portion, for my part I was always against the Cavaleers cause;

yet their persons are part peace before some of you scoffing *Ishmaelites*; I am sure you act contrary to the Scripture which bids you *Love your enemies, and doe as you would be done by*, and this Scripture you say you own; why then do you not practice it, and doe to the Cavaliers as the Prophet *Eliah* bid the King of *Israel* do to his enemies whom he had taken prisoners, *Set bread and water* (saith he) *before them, and send them to their master in peace.*

Come, make peace with the Cavaliers your enemies, and let the oppressed go free, and let them have a livelihood, and love your enemies, and doe to them, as you would have had them done to you if they had conquered you: Well, let them go in peace, and let love wear the Crown.

For I tell you, and your Preachers, that Scripture which saith, *The poor shall inherit the earth*, is really and materially to be fulfilled, for the Earth is to be restored from the bondage of sword proprietie, and it is to become a common Treasurie in reallitie to whole mankind, for this is the work of the true Saviour to doe, who is the true and faithfull Leveller even the Spirit and power of universall love, that is now rising to spread himself in the whole creation, who is the blessin, and will spread as far as the curse had spred to take it of, and cast him out, and who will set the creation in peace.

This powerfull Saviour will not set up his Kingdom nor rule his Creation with sword and fighting, as some think and fear, for he hath declared to you long since, that they that take the sword to save themselves shall perish with the sword.

But this shall be the way of his conquest, even as in the daies of the Beast, the whole world wondred after him, set him up, and was subject to him, and did persecute universall love, and made War against him and his Saints, and overcame them for a time.

Even so the Spirit of love and blessing shall arise and spread in mankind like the Sun from East to West, and by his inward power of love, light, and righteousness, shall let mankind see the abomination of the swordly Kingly power, and shall loath themselves in dust and ashes, in that they have owned and upheld him so long, and shall fall off from him, loath him and leave him.

And this shall be your miserie O you covetous oppressing Tyrants of the Earth, not only you great self-seeking powers of *England*, but you powers of all the World, The people shall all fall off from you, and you shall fall on a sudden like a great tree that is undermined at the root. And you powers of *England* you cannot say another day but you had warning, this falling of is begun already, divisions shall tear and torter you, till you submit to Communitie; O come in, come in to righteousness that you may find peace.

You or some of you hate the name *Leveller*, and the chiefest of you are afraid and ashamed to own a *Leveller*, and you laugh and jeer at them; Well, laugh out poor blind souls, the people and common Souldiers both lets you alone, but they laugh in their hearts at you, and yet desire that you did know the things that concern your peace.

The time is very neer that the people generally shall loath and be ashamed of your Kingly power, in your preaching, in your Laws, in your Councels, as now you are ashamed of the *Levellers*; I tell you Jesus Christ who is that powerfull Spirit of Love is the head *Leveller*, and *as he is lifted up, hee will draw all men after him*, and leave you naked and bare, and make you ashamed in your selves, his appearance will be with power; therefore Kisse the Son O ye Rulers of the earth, least his anger fall upon you. The wounds of Conscience within you from him shall be sharper then the wounds made by your sword, he shook heaven and earth when *Moses* Law was cast out, but he will shake heaven and earth now to purpose much more, and nothing shall stand but what is lovely; be wise, scorn not the Councell of the poor, least you be whipt with your own rod.

This great Leveller, Christ our King of righteousness in us, shall cause men to beat their swords into plowshares, and spears into pruning hooks, and nations shall learn war no more, and every one shall delight to let each other enjoy the pleasures of the earth, and shall hold each other no more in bondage; then what will become of your power? truly he must be cast out for a murtherer; and I pittie you for the torment your spirit must go through, if you be not fore-armed, as you are abundantly forewarned from all places; but I look upon you as part of the creation who must be restored, and the Spirit may give you wisedom to forsee a danger, as he hath admonished divers of your rank already to leave those high places, and to lie quiet and wait for the breakings forth of the powerfull day of the Lord. Farewel, once more. Let *Israel* go free.

A BILL OF ACCOUNT OF THE MOST REMARKABLE SUFFERINGS THAT THE DIGGERS HAVE MET WITH FROM THE GREAT RED DRAGONS POWER SINCE *APRIL 1. 1649*. WHICH WAS THE FIRST DAY THAT THEY BEGAN TO DIGGE, AND TO TAKE POSSESSION OF THE COMMONS FOR THE POOR ON *GEORGE-HILL* IN *SURREY*.

1 *The first time, divers of the Diggers were carried Prisoners into* Walton *Church, where some of them were struck in the Church by the bitter Professors and rude Multitude; but after some time freed by a Justice.*

2 *They were fetched by above a hundred rude people, whereof* John Taylor *was the Leader, who took away their Spades, and some of them they never had again: and carried them first to Prison at* Walton, *and then to a Justice at* Kingstone, *who presently dismissed them.*

3 *The Dragonly enemy pulled down a House which the Diggers had built upon* George-Hill, *and cut their Spades and Howes to pieces.*

4 *Two Troops of Horse were sent from the General to fetch us before the Councel of War, to give Account of our Digging.*

5 *We had another House pulled down, and our Spades cut to pieces.*

6 *One of the Diggers had his head sore wounded, and a Boy beaten, and his Cloathes taken from him: divers being by.*

7 *We had a Cart and Wheels cut in pieces, and a Mare cut over the back with a Bill when we went to fetch a Load of Wood from* Stoak-Common,[13] *to build a House upon* George-Hill.

8 *Divers of the Diggers were beaten upon the* Hill *by* William Star *and* John Taylor, *and by men in womens apparel, and so sore wounded, that some of them were fetched home in a Cart.*

9 *We had another House pulled down, and the Wood they carried to* Walton *in a Cart.*

10 *They Arrested some of us, and some they cast into Prison; and from others they went about to take away their Goods, but that the Goods proved another mans, which one of the Diggers was Servant to.*

11 *And indeed at divers times besides we had all our Corn spoyled; for the Enemy was so mad, that they tumbled the Earth up and down, and would suffer no Corn to grow.*

12 *Another Cart and Wheels was cut to pieces, and some of our Tooles taken by force from us, which we never had again.*

13 *Some of the Diggers were beaten by the Gentlemen, the Sheriff looking on, and afterwards Five of them were carried to* White-Lion *Prison, and kept there about 5 weeks and then let out.*

14 *The Sheriff with the Lords of Mannors and Souldiers standing by, caused two or three poor men to pull down another House: and divers things were stoln from them.*

15 *The next day two Souldiers and two or three Country-men sent by Parson* Platt, *pulled down another House, and turned a poor old man and his wife out of doors to lie in the field on a cold night.*

And this is the last hitherto; and so you Priests as you were the last that had a hand in our persecution, so it may be that Misery may rest in your hand; for assure your selves, God in Christ will not be mocked by such Hypocrites that pretend to be his neerest and deerest Servants as you do, and yet will not suffer his hungry, naked, and house-less members to live quiet by you in the Earth, by whose Blood and Monies in these Wars, you are in peace.

And now those Diggers that remain, have made little Hutches to lie in like Calf-cribs, and are cheerful; taking the spoyling of their Goods patiently, and rejoycing that they are counted worthy to suffer persecution for Righteousnesse sake: and they follow their work close, and have Planted divers Acres of Wheat and Rie, which is come up and promises a very fruitful crop, and Resolves to preserve it by all the diligence they can, and nothing shall make them slack but want of Food, which is not much now, they being all poor People, and having suffered so much in one expence or other since they began; for Poverty is their greatest burthen; and if any thing do break them from the Work, it will be that.

You Lordly Foes you will rejoycethis newes to hear and see;
Do so, go on; but wee'l rejoyce much more the Truth to see:
For by our hands truth is declar'd, and nothing is kept back;
Our faithfulness much joy doth bring, though victuals we may lack.
This tryal may our God see good, to try, not us, but you;
That your profession of the Truth, may prove either false or true.

And these are the Troubles and Persecutions that the Diggers have gone through since they began, besides many particular abuses from rude Spirits, and multitudes of slanders, lyes, and bad names, that the mouths of the scoffing *Ishmaelites* are filled with, and the secret enmity that hath come from close Hypocrites, that goe for great Professors.

But now Profession, thou art tryed
to purpose, all shall see,
And verbal talk it will appear
a Devil for to be:
For actions pure, holds forth the life

of God and Christ most dear:
And false Dissembling now must die,
if Scriptures you will hear;
You preaching men if Truth you'l own,
see Truth be acted to,
Or else to Christ you will appear
to be his mortal foe.
Scribes, Pharisees, and the Theif,
that Judas *was by name,*
Great preachers were, but for no deeds,
the Truth they much did stain:
No deeds you'l say! Yes, that they had:
its true they had indeed;
But what deeds were they you can see?
no herb, but stinking weed:
For Persecution ever was
the Work that came from them,
And deadly foes they ever were,
to Christ, and righteous men.

And here I end, having put my Arm as far as my strength will go to advance Righteousness: I have Writ, I have Acted, I have Peace: and now I must wait to see the Spirit do his own work in the hearts of others, and whether *England* shall be the first Land, or some others, wherein Truth shall sit down in triumph.

But O *England, England*, would God thou didst know the things that belong to thy peace before they be hid from thine eyes: The Spirit of Righteousness hath striven with thee, and doth yet strive with thee, and yet there is hope. Come in thou *England*, submit to Righteousness before the voice go out, my Spirit shall strive no longer with Flesh; and let not Covetousnesse make thee oppress the poor.

We have Declared our Reasons for our Digging plentifully enough; and you Rulers of *England*, will you always be like deaf

Adders, &c? We have received many affronts from Lords of Mannors and their Servants divers times; yet nothing makes us be at a stand, Whether *England* shall be the first Land that shall fall off from the Beast, and set Righteousnesse upon the Throne, or no, but the late Action of the head of the Souldiery, in granting a party of Horse to come and weaken us.

Gentlemen of the Souldiery, be not offended, for you promised me in *Whitehal* Gallerie, that you would not meddle with us, but leave us to the Law of the Land, and the Country Gentlemen to deal with us, and so you did a long time, and we hope in time that love and patience will conquer our furious enemies.

Yet we understand which a little troubles us, yet content That the Generall gave his consent that the Souldiers should come to help to beat of the Diggers, and to pull down their Houses; it is true, the Souldiers with the Gentlemen our enemies came, and caused others to pull down our houses, but the Souldiers did not meddle, none but one, but expressed sorrow to see the Passages.

But though they were modest, and expressed tenderness, yet the Generals grant and the Souldiers presence was a great crush to our business; Gentlemen of the Army, we have spoke to you, we have appealed to the Parliament, we have declared our cause with all humilitie to you all, and we are Englishmen, and your friends that stuck to you in your miseries, and these Lords of Mannors that oppose us were wavering on both sides, yet you have heard them, and answered their request to beat us off, and yet you would not afford us an Answer.

Yet love and patience shall lie down and suffer; Let pride and covetousness stretch themselves upon their beds of ease, and forget the afflictions of *Joseph*, and persecute us for righteousness sake, yet we will wait to see the issue, the power of righteousness is our God; the globe runs round, the longest Sun-shine day ends in a dark night; and therefore to thee O thou King of righteousness we doe commit our cause; Judge thou between us and them that strive against us, and those that deal treacherously with thee and us, and doe thine own work, and help weak flesh in whom the Spirit is willing.

FINIS.

NOTES

1. The pamphlet itemizes the 'most remarkable sufferings' of the Digger colony over a hard winter. The Diggers wrote twice to Fairfax in December bringing his attention to the slander and rough treatment they had endured.

2. Many oaths and engagements had emanated from the New Model Army, for example *The Solemn Engagement of the Army* in 1647.

3. John Platt, lord of the manor of Cobham, where the Diggers re-located around August 1649.

4. Debenters: certificates of wages owing. There was a booming trade in former crown land, royalist estates, and dean and chapter lands.

5. See the following text, *A Vindication Of Those Whose endeavours is only to make the Earth a common treasury, called Diggers*.

6. Charles II, so called: provisionally recognised by the Scots on 5 February 1649 and in talks with them through 1649 and early 1650 concerning the terms of an alliance.

7. Kent like many other counties had seen royalist uprisings in 1648. The Kentish rebels captured several castles and even warships before Fairfax broke the main force at Maidstone on 1 June. A fortnight earlier, 3,000 armed men had descended on Westminster Hall from Surrey with a petition for restoration of the king. The army was called in; there were several fatalities.

8. Parliament abolished wardship and the Court of Wards in 1646, so that assembled landowners could convert land held from the king by feudal tenure – and vulnerable to royal predation – into unassailable freehold property.

9. The monarchy was abolished on 17 March 1649; the House of Lords followed two days later.

10. Corns, et al. (v. ii, pp. 155–6n) comment that while a direct translation ('Not by arms, but through death, did Jesus conquer demons') does not fit the verse, 'it is impossible to say whether this was because [Winstanley] did not fully understand the Latin. His use of biblical texts was often equally free.'

11. Landlords could impose 'entry fines' on copyholders and force eviction for non-payment. Parliament's prompt abolition of wardship protected landowners from similar sharp practice by the king: see n8.

12. This may have been the occasion Winstanley delivered the two further Digger letters to Fairfax: see n1.

13. In the neighbouring parish of Stoke d'Abernon.

A

VINDICATION

OF THOSE,

Whose endeavours is only to make
the Earth a common treasury, called

DIGGERS.

OR,

Some Reasons given by them against the
immoderate use of creatures, or the excessive
community of women called Ranting;
or rather Renting.[1]

First those that are called Diggers; doe looke upon the Ranting Practise, to be a Kingdome without the man; which moth and rust doe, may, and will corrupt; and which thieves may break through and steale away; It is Kingdome that lies in objects; As in the outward enjoyment of meat, drinke, pleasures, and women; so that the man within can have no quiet rest, unlesse he enjoy those outward objects in excesse; all which are vanishable. Therefore it is the Devills Kingdome of darknesse, and not the Kingdome of heaven nor true peace within.

Secondly, this outward life, in the abundant eating and drinking, and actuall community with variety of women, is the onely life of the five sences, which is the life of the Beast, or living flesh; And fights against reason, who is the seed or tree of life, or the righteous man that is within. For when the sensitive power, which is the sonne of bondage rules, then Reason which is the sonne of freedome, is trod under foot and in the absence thereof the whole body, whole Families, nay, whole Nations are distempered; But when Reason rules in the house or heart, not suffering the sences to runne into excesse in any action: then the whole body enjoyes quiet rest and peace. Therefore that immoderate ranting practise of the Sences, is not the true life of peace.

Thirdly, the Ranting practise is the proper Kingdome of Covetousnesse, or King Lust of the flesh, which is the Kingdome of darknesse, full of unreasonablenesse, madnesse and confusion; it is the land of darknesse, bringing forth nothing but miserie to the Inhabitants thereof, for,

Fourthly, it is destructive to the body, house, or Temple, wherein Reason, or the spirituall power dwells; it brings diseases, infirmenesse, weaknesses and rottenesse upon the body, and so ruines the house about the mans eares, that he cannot live in quiet peace; for diseases of body causes sorrow of mind. And as moderation in any action brings peace, so excesse brings diseases and death. Therefore the unrationall ranting practise is not the life of rightnesse, nor peace.

Fifthly it brings vexation to the mind or man within for when you want your delight in the excessive copolation with Women, and in the super abundant eating and drinking, which is the wastfull spending of the Treasures of the Earth. As the Ranting practise is, Then Angar, rage and varietie of vexations possesses the mind, and inflames their harts to quarreling, killing, burning houses or Corne, or to such like destructivenesse.

Sixtly, The Ranting practise is a peace breaker; it breaks the peace in Families, and rents in peeces mankind, for where true Love hath united a man and woman to be Husband and Wife, and they live in peace, when this Ranting power or king lust of the flesh comes in, he seperates those very friends, causing both sides to run into the Sea of confusion, madnesse and distruction, to leave each other, to leave their Children, and to live in discontent each with other.

It pretends love to all men and women. But yet he is a beast that respects persons; for the richest and fairest must be his associate.

Seaventhly, This excesse of Feminine society, hinders the pure and naturall Generation of man, and spills the seed in vaine, and instead of a healthfull groth of mankind it produces weaknesse and much infirmnesse, through immoderate heat; so that either the Mother hath much more paine in child bearing, or els the child is fild with such infirmnesse, that it proves a burden to the Mother or nurse, or through deseases he brings with him into the world he proves either not long lived, or a foole, or else a sickly weakly thing that is a burden to himselfe: So that this moderat Ranting, is not a healthfull builder up of the creation man, but a violent waster and destroyer of the health and strength of man. This false generating fire, is the foundation of much lamentation for children begotten through this forced immoderat heat of lust, proves, furious, and full of rage, it is a breeder of much distemper, Warres, and quarrells; It is one cause if not the chief of the rising up of the hairie man, which is a destroyer of himselfe and others. And the mother and child begotten in this manner, is like to have the worst of it, for the men will be gone and leave them; and regard them no more then other women, like a Bull that begets a Calfe, that never takes care neither for Cow nor Calfe, after he hath had his pleasure. Therefore you women beware, for this ranting practise is not the restoring, but the destroying power of the creation.

Eighthly, The Ranting practise, is the support of Idlenesse, for they that are, the Sons and Daughters of that unrationall power, neither can nor will work, but live idle, like wandering bussy bodies, expressing and cheating others, that are simple and of a civil flexible nature, so that by seeking their owne freedom they imbondage others which is the selfish, but not the universall Love, for true Love seeks the preservation of others as of one selfe, or else for want of food and rayment, through an inward proud sullennesse, either sterves their owne bodies, or else through an inward rage endeavours the ruine of others.

Ninthly, This Ranting power, or god, is full of sutletie to deceive others of what they earn, and is a nurse of hardnesse of heart against others, when he hath deceived them, for this is his nature, to get what he can from others, labours to eat up other and made them poore, and then to laugh and rejoyce in others poverty.

Tenthly, The Ranting power, would make this Covenant with all men, to put out their eyes, or suffer him quiety to put them out, and to see by his eyes, and to walk by his legges and then he calls them high lighted creatures, otherwise he tells them they live belowe them, and is in the dark, and rather then proud civility would be counted ignorant, it will yeeld, and first stands looking and saying, I can say nothing against this ranting practise, and then afterwards yeelds, and then is ensnared and taken by the suttle devouring Ranting Beast. But now he that obeys reasons, Law of righteousnesse within, shall escape that snare.

Eleventhly, This Ranting power, is the resurrection of the uncleane doggish beastly nature, it is the resurrection of the filth, unrighteouse power in all his branches, and it is high now, but will rise higher, for it must rise to the hight to shew himselfe a compleat man of darknesse, that he may come to judgement and so be cast out of heaven, That is out of mankinde.

For as he is upon his resurrection, so the man of pure life, reason, and righteousnesse, is upon his resurrection too. Who is rising to purge and to restore the creation, and to set it downe in peace. And these two men, one of Light, and the other of darknesse, now strives with great vehemencie; the sonnes of darknesse may live in their vanishable peace and tread the sonnes of light under feet but the sonnes of peace shall rise up, and take peace from the Earth.

There is only two things, I must speak as an Advice in Love

First, let every one that intends to live in peace, set themselves with dilligent labour to Till, Digge, and Plow, the Common and barren Land, to get their bread with righteous moderat working, among a moderat minded people, this prevents the evill of Idlenesse, and the danger of the Ranting power.

Secondly, Let none goe about to suppresse that ranting power by their punishing hand, for it is the work of the Righteous and rationall spirit within not thy hand without that must suppresse it; But if thou wilt needs be punishing: Then see thou be without sinne thy selfe, and then cast the first Stone, at the Ranter; Let not sinners punish others for sin, but let the power of thy Reason and righteous action, shame and so beat downe their unrationall actings.

Would thou live in peace; Then look to thy own wayes, mind thy owne Kingdome within, trouble not at the unrational government of other mens kingdomes without; Let every one alone, to stand and fall to their owne Master for thou being a sinner, and strives to suppresse sinners by force, thou wilt thereby but increase their rage, and thy owne trouble: but do thou keep close to the Law of righteous reason, and thou shalt presently see a returne of the Ranters: for that spirit within must shame them, and turne them, and pull them out of darknesse.

This I was moved to write, as a Vindication of the Diggers, who are slandered with the Ranting action: And my end is only to Advance the Kingdome of peace, in and among mankinde, which is and will be torne in peeces by the Ranting power, if reason do not kill this fine headed, or sencitive Beast.

All you that are meerly civill, and that are of a loving and flexible disposition wanting the strength of reason: and the life of universall love, leading you forth to seeke the peace and preservation of every single body, as of one's selfe; You are the People that are like to be tempted, and set upon and torne into peeces by this devouring Beast; the Ranting power.

Febr. this 20. 1 6 4 9.

Gerrard Winstanley.

Therefore know all yee Lasivious, feedars, or Sarvers of your own bellies, that ye are breeders of all foule filthy beastly and Abominable Children, which come into the world to preach to that Nation, where they appeare, what the first signe of filthy Sinne or lasivious feeding heats, begot for lasivious feeding, causeth lacivious acting which if they knew the resurrection or eternall Iudgement, they durst not act.

I am told there are some people goes up and downe in the Country among such as are friends to the Diggers gathering Monyes in their names. And they have a note wherein my name and divers others are subscribed. This is to certifie that I never subscribed my name to any such note. Neither have we that are called Diggers, received any money by any such Collections, therefore to prevent this Cheat: we desire if any are willing to cast a gift in, to further our work of Digging upon the Commons, that they would send it to our owne hands by some trustie friend of their owne.

March this 4th. 1649.

Your friend
Gerrard Winstanley.

FINIS.

NOTE

1. In the previous text, Winstanley had commented that 'there have some come among the Diggers that have caused scandall, but we dis-own their wayes'. On the Ranters see A. L. Morton, *The World of the Ranters*. The main part of this document is dated 20 February 1649, i.e. 1650, if the New Year is taken on 1 January rather than 25 March.

An Appeale to all Englishmen, to judge between Bondage and Freedome,

sent from those that began to digge upon George Hill
in Surrey; but now are carrying on, that publick work
upon the little Heath in the Parish of COBHAM, neare unto
GEORGE Hill, wherein it appeares, that the work of digging
upon the Commons, is not onely warranted by Scripture,
but by the Law of the Common-wealth of England likewise.[1]

BEhold, behold, all *Englishmen*, The Land of *England* now is your free Inheritance: all *Kingly* and Lordly entanglements are declared against, by our *Army* and *Parliament*. The *Norman* power is beaten in the field, and his head is cut off. And that oppressing *Conquest* that hath raigned over you by *King* and *House of Lords*, for about 600. yeares past, is now cast out, by the *Armies* Swords, the *Parliaments* Acts and Lawes, and the *Common-wealths* Engagement.[2]

Therefore let not *Sottish* covetousnesse in the *Gentrey*, deny the poore or younger Brethren, their just Freedom to build and plant Corne upon the common wast Land: nor let slavish fear, possese the hearts of the poor, to stand in awe of the *Norman* Yoake any longer, seeing it is broke. Come, those that are free within, turn your Swords into Plough-shares, and Speares into pruning-hookes, and take *Plow* and *Spade* and break up the Common Land, build your Houses, sow Corne, and take possession of your own Land, which you have recovered out of the hands of the *Norman* oppressour.

The common Land hath lain unmanured all the dayes of his *Kingly* and *Lordly* power over you, by reason whereof, both you and your Fathers, (many of you) have been burthened with poverty. And that Land which would have been fruitfull with

Corne, hath brought forth nothing but heath, mosse, furseys, and the curse, according to the words of the Scriptures: *A fruitful Land is made barren, because of the unrighteousnesse of the People that ruled therein, and would not suffer it to be planted, because they would keep the Poor under bondage, to maintain their own Lordly Power, and conquering covetousnesse.*

But what hinders you now? will you be slaves and beggers still, when you may be Freemen? will you live in straits, and die in poverty, when you may live comfortably? will you allwayes make a profession of the words of *Christ* and *Scripture*: the sum whereof is this. *Do as you would be done unto, and live in love?* And now it is come to the point of fulfilling that righteous Law: wil you not rise up & act, I do not mean act by the sword, for that must be left? But come, take *Plow* & *Spade*, build & plant, & make the wast Land fruitfull, that there may be no begger nor idle person among us; for if the wast Land of *England* were manured by her Children, it would become in a few yeares the richest, the strongest, and flourishing Land in the World, and all *Englishmen* would live in peace and comfort; And this freedom is hindered by such as yet are full of the *Norman* base blood, who would be Free men themselves, but would have all others bond men and Servants, nay slaves to them.

The Law of the *Scriptures* gives you a full freedom to the Earth, and makes Man-kind free in all his Members; *for God, or the creating spirit, is no respector of persons.*

The *Ministers* who preache up the Law of the *Scriptures*, plead for their Freedom in the Earth, and say, *The Labourer is worthy of his hire.* But these *Ministers*, are faulty in two things. First, They will set themselves to work, in that they will run before they be sent, and then force the People by the power of the Sword Law, to give them wages, or Labourers hire. And they will not take 12 *d.* a day as other Labourers have, but they will compel 100 *l.* or more to be paid them yearly. Secondly, They lay claime to Heaven after they are dead, and yet they require their Heaven in this World too, and grumble mightily against the People that will not give them a large temporal maintenance. And yet they tell the poor People, that they must be content with their Poverty, and they shall have Heaven hereafter. But why may not we have our Heaven here, (that is, a comfortable livelihood in the Earth) And Heaven hereafter too, as well as you, *God is no respecter of Persons*?

Therefore say we, while we have bodies that must be fed and cloathed, let us have Earth to plant, to raise food and rayment by our labours, according to the Law of our Creation, and let us live like men of your own Image and forme:

But if you say, that this is onely old *Adams* condition to look after the Earth; but the new *Adam Christ*, lookes after Heaven above, and mindes not the Earth. As one publick Minister told us, why truly then we say, you make old *Adam* who brings in the curse to be more rational and tender over our bodies; then the second *Adam Christ* who brings in the blessing to all Nations.

But if it be old *Adams* condition to desire a Livelihood as we are men, and to live free from straits: Then I would have all those *Ministers* to cast aside their 100 *l.* or 200 *l.* a yeare, and go and beg their food and rayment of others, and expect their Heaven hereafter, as they bid poor men do.

But you covetous blind deceivers, know this, that as old *Adam* brings *Man-kind* into bondage and straits, so the second *Adam* brings *Man-kind* into Freedom, plenty and peace, here in this Earth while bodies are living upon earth: therefore he is said to be the joy of all Nations here on Earth, and the restorer of the whole Creation, that groanes under bondage here on Earth.

Well *Englishmen*, The Law of the *Scriptures*, gives you a free and full Warrant to plant the Earth, and to live comfortably and in love, doing as you would be done by: And condemns that covetous Kingly and Lordly power of darkness in men, that makes some men seeke their freedom in the Earth, and to deny others that freedom. And the *Scriptures* do establish this Law, to

cast out *Kingly* and *Lordly* self-willed and oppressing power, and
to make every Nation in the World a free *Common-wealth*. So
that you have the *Scriptures* to protect you, in making the Earth
a common Treasury, for the comfortable Livelihood of your
bodies, while you live upon Earth.

Secondly, You have both what the *Army* and *Parliament*
have done to protect you, as it will appeare by this graduall
consideration.

First, *King Charles* was the successour of the *Norman* Conquest,
and raigned as a Conquerour over *England*, for his Power held
the Land from us, and would rather see us die in poverty, or
hang us up, then suffer us to plant the *Commons* for our livelihood. And *Lords of Mannours* hold claiming to their *Copy-holds*,
and to the *Commons*, under or from the *King*: so that *Kings* and
Lordly power, is the power of the *Conquest* over the people.

Secondly, Our *Common-wealths Army* have fought against the
Norman Conquest, and have cast him out, and keepes the field.
By vertue of which victory, both the Title of the *King*, and the
Title of *Lords* of *Mannors* to the Land as *Conquerors* is lost. And
the Land now is as free to others as to them; yea, according to
Davids Law, to them that staid at home with the stuffe, as to
them that went out to warre: And by this victory, *England* is
made a free *Common-wealth*. And the common Land belongs
to the younger Brother, as the Enclosures to the elder Brother,
without restraint.

Then Thirdly, The *Parliament*, since this victory, have made
an *Act* or *Law*, to make *England* a free *Common-wealth*. And by
this *Act* they have set the People free, from *King* and *House of
Lords* that ruled as *Conquerors* over them, and have abolished
their self will and murdering Lawes, with them that made them.

Likewise they have made another *Act* or *Law*, to cast out
Kingly Power, wherein they free the People from yielding obe-
dience to the *King*, or to any that holds claiming under the *King*:
Now all *Lords* of *Mannours*, Tything Priests and impropriators,

hold claiming or Title under the *King*, but by this Act of *Parliament* we are freed from their Power.

Then lastly, The *Parliament* have made an *Engagement*, to maintain this present *Common-wealths* Government, comprised within those 2. *Acts* or *Lawes* against *King* and *House of Lords*. And calles upon all Officers, Tenants, and all sort of People to subscribe to it, declaring that those that refuse to subscribe, shall have no priviledge in the *Common-wealth* of *England*, nor protection from the Law.[3]

Now behold all *Englishmen*, that by vertue of these 2. Lawes, and the *Engagement*, the Tenants of Copyholds, are freed from obedience to their Lords of *Mannors*,[4] and all poor People may build upon, and plant the *Commons*, and the *Lords* of *Mannours* break the Lawes of the Land & the *Engagement*, & still uphold the *Kingly* and *Lordly Norman* Power, if they hinder them, or seek to beat them of from planting the *Commons*.

Neither can the *Lords* of *Mannors* compell their Tenants of Copy-holds, to come to their *Court-Barons*, nor to be of their *Juries*, nor take an Oath to be true to them, nor to pay fines, Heriots, quit-rent, nor any homage, as formerly, while the King and Lords were in their power. And if the Tenants stand up to maintain their Freedom, against their *Lords* oppressing power, the Tenants forfeit nothing, but are protected by the *Laws* and *Engagement* of the Land.

And if so be, that any poor men build them houses, and sow Corne upon the *Commons*, the *Lords* of *Mannors* cannot compell their Tenants to beat them of: And if the Tenants refuse to beat them off, they forfeit nothing, but are protected by the *Lawes* and *Engagement* of the Land. But if so be, that any fearfull or covetous Tenant, do obey their *Court-Barons*, and will be of their *Jury*, and will still pay Fines, Heriots, quit-Rents, or any homage as formerly, or take new Oaths, to be true to their *Lords*, or at the Command of their *Lords*, do beat the poor men off from planting the *Commons*; then they have broke the *Engagement*, and the

Law of the Land, and both Lords and Tenants are conspiring to uphold or bring in the *Kingly* and *Lordly* Power again, and declare themselves enemies to the Army, and to the Parliament, and are traytors to the *Commonwealth* of *England*. And if so be they are to have no protection of the *Lawes*, that refused to tak the *Engagement*, surely they have lost their protection by breaking their *Engagement*, and stand lyable to answer for this their offence, to their great charge and trouble, if any will prosecute against them. Therefore you *English men*, whether Tenants or labouring men, do not enter into a new bond of slavery, now you are come to the point that you may be free, if you will stand up for freedom; for the Army hath purchased your freedom. The Parliament hath declared for your freedom, and all the Lawes of the *Commonwealth* are your protection, so that nothing is wanting on your part, but courage and faithfulness, to put those Lawes in execution, and to take possesion of your own Land, which the *Norman* Power took from you, and hath kept from you about 600. yeares, which you have now recovered out of his hand. And if any say that the old Lawes and Customes of the Land, are against the Tenant and the poor, and intitle the Land onely to the *Lords* of *Mannours* still, I answer, all the old Lawes are of no force, for they are abolished, when the *King* and *House* of *Lords* were cast out. And if any say, I but the Parl: made an Act to establish the old Lawes, I answer, this was to prevent a sudden rising upon the cutting off the *Kings* head; but afterwards they made these 2. Lawes, to cast out *Kingly* Power, and to make *England* a *Commonwealth*. And they have confirmed these 2. by the *Engagement*, which the People now generally do own and subscribe: therefore by these Acts of freedom, they have abolished that Act that held up bondage. Well, by these you may see your freedom, and we hope the *Gentry* hereafter, wil cheat the poor no longer of their Land, and we hope, the *Ministers* hereafter will not tell the poor they have no right to the Land, for now the Land of *England*, is and ought to a common

Treasury to all *English men*, as the severall portions of the Land of *Canaan*, were the common Livelihood to such and such a Tribe; both to elder and younger Brother, without respect of persons. If you deny this, you deny the Scriptures. And now we shall give you some few encouragements out of many, to move you to stand up for your freedom in the Land, by acting with *Plow* and *Spade* upon the *Commons*.

1. *By this meanes within a short time, there will be no begger nor idle person in* England, *which will be the glory of* England, *and the glory of that Gospel, which* England *seemes to professe in words.* 2. *The wast and common Land being improved, will bring in plenty of all Commodities, and prevent famine, and pull down the prizes of Corne, to* 12 d. *a Bushel, or lesse.* 3. *It will prove* England *to be the first of Nations, or the tenth part of the City* Babylon, *which falls off from the covetous beastly Government first; and that sets the Crown of freedom upon Christs head, to rule over the Nations of the world, and to declare him to be the joy and blessing of all Nations. This should move all Governours to strive, who shall be the first that shall cast down their Crownes, Scepters, and Government at Christs feete, and they that will not give Christ his own glory, shall be shamed.* 4. *This Commonwealths freedom, will unite the hearts of* Englishmen *together in love so that if a forraign enemy endeavour to come in, we shall all with joynt consent rise up to defend our Inheritance, and shall be true one to another. Whereas now, the poor see, if they fight, and should conquer the Enemy yet either they or their Children are like to be slaves still, for the Gentrey will have all. And this is the cause why many run away and faile our Armies in the time of need. And so through the Gentries hardness of heart against the poor: The Land may be left to a forraigne enemy, for want of the poores love sticking to them; for say they, we can as well live under a forraign enemy working for day wages, as under our own brethren, with whom we ought to have equal freedom by the Law of righteousness.* 5. *This freedom in planting the common Land, will prevent robbing, stealing, and murdering, and Prisons will not so mightily be filled with Prisoners; and thereby we*

shall prevent that hart breaking spectacle of seeing so many hanged every Sessions as there are. And surely this imprisoning and hanging of men is the Norman *power still, and cannot stand with the freedom of the Commonwealth, nor warranted by the Engagement; for by the Lawes and Engagement of the Commonwealth, none ought to be hanged, nor put to death for other punishments may be found out. And those that do hang or put to death their fellow* Englishmen, *under colour of Lawes, do break the Lawes and the Engagement by so doing, and casts themselves from under the protection of the Commonwealth, and are traytors to* Englands *freedom, and upholders of the Kingly murdering power. 6. This freedom in the common earth, is the poorers right by the Law of Creation and equity of the Scriptures, for the earth was not made for a few, but for whole Mankind, for God is no respecter of Persons.*

* Now these few Considerations, we offer to all *England*, and we appeale to the judgement of all rational and righteous men; whether this we speak, be not that substantiall Truth brought forth into action, which Ministers have preached up, and all religious men have made profession of; for certainly, God who is the King of righteousness, is not a God of words only, but of deedes; for it is the badge of hypocrisie, for a man to say, and not to do. Therefore we leave this with you all, having peace in our hearts, by declaring faith fully to you, this light that is in us, and which we do not onely speake and write, but which we do easily act & practise. Likewise we write it, as a Letter of congratulation, and encouragement to our dear fellow *Englishmen*, that have begun to digge upon the Commons, thereby taking possession of their freedom in *Willinborow* in *Northamptonshire*: And at *Cox Hall* in *Kent*[5] waiting to see the chains of slavish fear to break and fall off from the hearts of others in other Countries, till at last the whole Land is filled with the knowledge & righteousness of the restoring power, which is *Christ* himself, *Abrahams* seed, who will spread himself til he become the joy of all Nations.

Jerard Winstanley.
Richard Maidley.   *John Hayman.*
Thomas James.   *William Hitchcock.*
John Dickins.   *Henry Hancocke.*
John Palmer.   *John Barry.*
John South, Elder.   *Thomas Starre.*
Nathaniel Holcomb.   *Thomas Adams.*
Thomas Edcer.   *John Coulton.*
Henry Barton.   *Thomas South.*
John South.   *Robert Sayear.*
Jacob Heard.   *Daniel Freland.*
Thomas Barnat.   *Robert Draper.*
Anthony Wren.   *Robert Coster.*

And divers others that were not present when this went to the Presse.

March, 26.
1650.

NOTES

1. Published on 26 March 1650 partly to convey 'congratulation and encouragement' to other Digger colonies: one in Kent, the other in Wellingborough, Northamptonshire. The latter group had issued *A Declaration of the Grounds and Reasons. . .* for their own initiative on or before 12 March.
2. The Engagement to be 'true and faithful to the Commonwealth of England, as it is now established, without a King or House of Lords' was published by Parliament on 2 January 1650. All adult males were required to take it. Winstanley did so in Cobham on 16 March, along with other Diggers.
3. The Act for Subscribing the Engagement (2 January 1650) authorized judges 'to stop all further proceedings' in cases where the plaintiff had not taken the Engagement. See n2.
4. Winstanley might wish away the insecurities of copyhold tenure, but the landowners in Parliament blocked any reform. See p. 136, n11.
5. Probably a misspelling: no such place as Cox Hall, Kent, is known, though there are places in the county with similar names.

A LETTER TAKEN AT WELLINBOROUGH[1]

Thursday Aprill 4.

The true Copy of a letter taken at *Wellingborough* in Northamptonshire, with some men that were there apprehended for going about to incite people to digging, and under that pretence gathered mony of the Wel-affected for their assistance:

These are to certifie all that are Friends to universall freedom, and that looke upon the Digging and Planting the Commons to be the first springing up of freedome, to make the earth a common treasury that every one may enjoy food and rayment freely by his labour upon the earth, without paying rents or homage to any fellow creature of his own kind, that every one may be delivered from the tyranny of the conquering power; and so rise up out of that bondage to enjoy the benefit of his Creation: This I say is to certifie all such that those men that have begun to lay the first stone in the foundation of this freedome; by digging upon Georges Hill, and the Common called Little heath in *Cobham*, in regard of the great opposition hitherto from the enemy, by Reason whereof they lost the last summers work, yet through inward faithfullnesse to advance freedome they keep the field still and have planted divers Acres of Corn and built 4. houses, and now this season time goes on digging, endeavouring to plant as much as they can; but in regard of poverty their work is like to flagge and droppe: Therefore if the hearts of any be stirred up to cast any thing into this treasury, to buy Victualls to keep the men alive, and to buy Corn to cast into the ground it will keep alive the beginning of publique Freedom to the whole Land, which otherwise is ready to die again for want of help; And if you hear hereafter that there was a people appeared to stand up to advance publique freedome, and strugled with the opposing power of the Land for that they begin to let them alone, and yet these men and their publique work was crushed, because they wanted assistance of food and Corne to keep them alive; I say if you heare this it will be trouble to you when it is too late, that you had monies in your hands, and would not part with any of it to purchase freedome, therefore you deservedly Grone under Tyranny and no Saviour appeares; but let your Reason weigh the excellency of this worke of digging the Commons, and I am sure you will cast in something.

And because there were some treacherous persons drew up a note and subscribed our names to it, and by that moved some friends to give mony to this work of ours, when as we know of no such note, nor subscribed our hands to any, nor never received any money from such Collection.

Therefore to prevent such a Cheat, I have mentioned a word or two in the end of a Printed Book against that treachery,[2] that neither we nor our Friends may be cheated: And I desire, if any be willing to communicate of their substance unto our worke, that they would make a Collection among themselves, and send that mony to *Cobham* to the Diggers owne hands, by some trusty friend of your owne, and so neither you nor we shall be cheated.

The Bearers hereof *Thomas Heaydon*, and *Adam Knight*, can relate by word of mouth largely the condition of the Diggers and their work and so we leave this to you to doe as you are moved.

Iacob Heard, Io: South junior, *Henry Barto, Tho: Barnard, Tho: Adams, Will Hitchcoke, Anthony Wrea, Robert Draper, William Smith, Robert Coster, Gerrard Winstanley, Io: South, Tho: Heydon, Io: Palmer, Tho: South, Henry Handcocke, Io: Batt, Dan: Freland, Io: Hayman, Robert Sawyer, Tho: Starre, Tho: Edcer,* Besides their Wives and Children, and many more if there were food for them.

A Copy of their travels that were taken with the four men at Wellingborow. *Out of* Buckinghamshire *into* Surry, *from* Surry *to* Middlesex, *from thence to* Hartfordshire, *to* Bedfordshire, *again to* Buckinghamshire, *so to* Barkeshire, *and then to* Surry, *thence to* Middlesex, *and so to* Hartfordshire, *and to* Bedforshire, *thence into* Huntingdonshire, *from thence to* Bedfordshire, *and so into* Northamptonshire, *and there they were Apprehended.*

They visited these towns to promote the Businesse. Colebrook, Hanworth, Hounslow, Harowhill, Watford, Redburn, Dunstable, Barton, Amersley, Bedford, Kempson, North Crawly, Cranfield, Newport, Stony-Stratford, Winslow, Wendover, Wickham, Windsor, Cobham, London, Whetston, Mine, Wellin, Dunton, Putney, Royston, St. Needs, Godmanchester, Wetne, Stanton, Warbays, Kimolton, *from* Kimolton *to* Wellingborow.[3]

NOTES

1. Reproduced in a popular news-sheet, *A Perfect Diurnall* (1–8 April 1650). Winstanley's Diggers are by now 'like to flagge and droppe'. They were dispersed shortly after this letter was published.
2. See *A Vindication Of Those Whose endeavours is only to make the Earth a common treasury, called Diggers*, above.
3. On the wider Digger network see the Foreword and Hill, *The World Turned Upside Down*, pp. 124–128.